MORNING
AFTER THE
REVOLUTION

T

MORNING AFTER THE REVOLUTION

Dispatches from the Wrong Side of History

NELLIE BOWLES

THESIS

Thesis
An imprint of Penguin Random House LLC
penguinrandomhouse.com

Most Thesis books are available at a discount when purchased in quantity
for sales promotions or corporate use. Special editions, which include
personalized covers, excerpts, and corporate imprints, can be created when
purchased in large quantities. For more information, please call (212)
572-2232 or e-mail specialmarkets@penguinrandomhouse.com. Your local
bookstore can also assist with discounted bulk purchases using the Penguin
Random House corporate Business-to-Business program. For assistance in
locating a participating retailer, e-mail B2B@penguinrandomhouse.com.

Portions of "A Utopia, If You Can Keep It" were previously published in
different form in "Abolish the Police? Those Who Survived the Chaos
in Seattle Aren't So Sure" in *The New York Times*, August 7, 2020.

Portions of "Masked Vigilantes Have Always Saved the World" were previously
published in different form in "Some Protests Against Police Brutality Take a More
Confrontational Approach" in *The New York Times*, September 21, 2020.

"The Failure of San Francisco" was published previously in different form as
"How San Francisco Became a Failed City" in *The Atlantic*, June 8, 2022.

Library of Congress Cataloging-in-Publication Data
Names: Bowles, Nellie, author.
Title: Morning after the revolution: 2020 and all that / Nellie Bowles.
Description: New York: Thesis, [2024]
Identifiers: LCCN 2023051205 (print) | LCCN 2023051206 (ebook) |
ISBN 9780593420140 (hardcover) | ISBN 9780593420157 (ebook)
Subjects: LCSH: Political culture—United States. | Progressivism
(United States politics) | Liberalism—United States. | United States—Politics
and government—2017-2021. | United States—Politics and government—2021–
Classification: LCC JK1726 .B69 2024 (print) | LCC JK1726 (ebook) |
DDC 320.973—dc23/eng/20240213
LC record available at https://lccn.loc.gov/2023051205
LC ebook record available at https://lccn.loc.gov/2023051206

Printed in the United States of America
1st Printing

BOOK DESIGN BY CHRIS WELCH

Some names and identifying characteristics have been changed to
protect the privacy of the individuals involved.

For my parents

Why the Term 'JEDI' Is Problematic for Describing Programs That Promote Justice, Equity, Diversity and Inclusion: They are a religious order of intergalactic police-monks, prone to (white) saviorism and toxically masculine approaches to conflict resolution (violent duels with phallic lightsabers, gaslighting by means of "Jedi mind tricks," etc.).

—Scientific American

Every year on Hummus Day, we like to share a fun little tidbit about Slack notifications. We realize now, this year, and specifically today, was not the right time to do that. Thank you to our @SlackHQ community for holding us accountable.

—Slack's official Twitter/X

Author's Note

I have changed names to protect private people from having some silly moment show up at the top of their Google. Where you find full names, those are real people.

Contents

Part III

MEN AND NON-MEN

Part IV

MORNING AFTER

Introduction

It's been a little while now, and it might be hard to remember that it was ever any different, but remember the pandemic and the rage. Remember many of us isolated, on our phones, on our computers, the stock market strangely rising as the government sent money flooding into the country. Remember that during all of this, there was a murder. The death was filmed. It went viral. And in the shadow of that pandemic and that murder and that money, American politics went berserk. Liberal intelligentsia, in particular, became wild, wild with rage and optimism, and fresh ideas from academia that began to reshape every part of society. The ideology that came shrieking in would go on to reshape

America in some ways that are interesting and even good, and in other ways that are appalling, but mostly in ways that are—I hate to say it—funny.

I remember a particularly hectic October afternoon in 2020.

The New York Times's celebrations of LGBTQIA+'s A-specific week (the week centering the asexual experience) coincided with International Pronouns Day, so my email was crowded by the time I walked the dog on my street, each house variously declaring in its window that "Black Lives Matter" and "No Justice No Peace" and listing things that the people In This Home Believe. One, a perfect nod to a cartoon, simply said: "Existence is Pain."

Later that day, Lowell High School, the most prestigious public school in San Francisco, abandoned all admissions requirements when the school board voted unanimously against them. It was an ostensible blow against white supremacy, but it was hard to square that with the working-class Asian teenagers in the room testifying to keep those admissions requirements. The school board got caught off mic calling them "racists," but the vote meant that more whites than ever would be admitted to Lowell. Strange, that.

The very same week, the city of my birth—my family has lived there for seven generations—passed the CAREN Act, a clever nod to the "Karen" meme, making racially motivated 911 calls a crime. And I noticed Harry and Meghan placed a crystal display in the Zoom background of their Montecito home, which somehow seemed relevant.

It was a new era. Liberals—those weak, wishy-washy compromisers, the hemmers and hawers—were out. Washing them away was the New Progressive. They came with politics built on the idea that people are profoundly good, denatured only by capitalism, by colonialism and whiteness and heteronormativity. It was a heady, beautiful philosophy.

The police could be abolished because people are kind and—once rescued from poverty and racism—wouldn't hurt each other. Homeless addicts can set up long-term communities in public parks because they absolutely will share space conscientiously with local families. Neighborhoods can be given over to protest movements because those protest movements know how to hold themselves accountable, and because city governments are old-fashioned and unnecessary when people are good. We don't need to authorize new housing because we can just ask young professionals not to move to a crowded town, and they'll of course understand. Gender dysphoric children should be given the medical interventions they ask for, at any age they ask, because those children know themselves perfectly. If a nonprofit leader says they are spending money on black lives, then that's what they're doing, and to ask for records is part of the problem.

The New Progressive knows that people are good and stable, reasonable and giving.

I was, in those days, in the days of Harry and Meghan and the crystal and the sense of universal goodness, a successful young reporter at *The New York Times,* a New Progressive doing the only job she had ever wanted.

"The truth is hard," the ads would say, and I believed in that

ad copy in an almost religious way. I felt I'd met destiny when I badged in to visit headquarters. Before I got the offer, I would look in the mirror and practice: "Hi, it's Nellie Bowles with *The New York Times*. Hi, Nellie Bowles, *New York Times*. Excuse me, a question from *The New York Times!*" In college I would look up the names of all the writers on the front page and try to figure out their paths to there, to that page.

Donald J. Trump was the president when I joined. Subscriptions were surging, and subscribers wanted something specific for their money: The *Times* would be the heart of resistance. We would champion the beautiful world that could be. My stories— fun riffs from Silicon Valley, investigations into creeps using video games to get kids, send-ups of conservative figures—fit right in. My work was cited in all-company meetings. I wrote big stories. I would go into the bureau on Sunday, and I never missed a happy hour.

Then something changed. The Black Lives Matter movement swept in, and as the movement grew, protests overtook the country and money came fast and some of the #Resistance started to get strange, but our job was to ignore all that. If parts of the movement were goofy it was *not funny*. My cohort took it as gospel when a nice white lady said that being On Time and Objectivity were white values, and this was a progressive belief, for example. But also it was important to note that there was no revolution happening and any backlash to it was bizarre and also vile. Because if it was happening, it was *good*. Even after Biden won and the threat of Trump faded, that tight narrative, that party line had to be held.

Everything was deathly serious. The letter X needed to be added to gender-neutral words to indicate extra gender-neutralness, extra pro-trans. Folks became folx. Groups that didn't want to be given new names were given them anyway, to show gender neutrality. Latino became Latinx. Otherwise, you were a monster.

Most of the new guard at the paper had come there for that revolution. They entered the building on a mission. They weren't there to tell dry news factoids so much as wield the pen for justice. It was a more beautiful vision of the role of journalism for such a beautiful time, more compelling for the writer and for the reader. Yes, it was a little confusing to do reporting for a place that was so sure everyone was good, except, of course, conservatives, who were very *very* bad and whose politics only come from hate. Asking for coherence is white supremacy. I figured it out. I loved my job.

New acronyms dropped and then had to be understood quickly or else. An announcement: "May 17 marks the International Day Against Homophobia, Biphobia, Interphobia, and Transphobia (IDAHOBIT), which celebrates LGBTQIA+ people globally and raises awareness to combat discrimination." Justin Trudeau says in October 2021: "People across the country are lighting candles to honor Indigenous women, girls, and 2SLGBTQQIA+ people who are missing or have been murdered." An acceptable alternative is: LGBTQQIP2SAA. There's DEIBJ (diversity, equity, inclusion, belonging, and justice) and BBIPOC (black, brown, indigenous, and [other] people of color).

No one was exempt from the revolution; all brands needed to

announce they were with the New Progressives or they were against us. For a few years, there was no brand in my life that didn't apologize for its past horrors or at least raise a fist against the cops. Our dog shelter posted for donations to Black Lives Matter. (I faved it, of course.) Seventh Generation, which makes my favorite toilet paper, posted: "We support defunding the police." Oreo's corporate account posted: "Trans people exist."

Pepé Le Pew was cut from the *Space Jam* movie for normalizing rape culture. *The Muppet Show* got a warning label, and the sexy M&M was butched up a bit. Some Dr. Seuss books were banned, and the Jane Austen House museum added details about her family's role in the slave trade. "There's a disturbing nexus of organic food and white supremacists," the business magazine *Fast Company* announced. "Ultimately, grocery shopping is the least avoidable and one of the most ethically compromised activities in our lives," *The New Republic* announced.

At various points, my fellow reporters at major news organizations told me roads and birds are racist. Voting is racist. Exercise is super racist. Worrying about plastics in the water is transphobic.

Brandeis University put out a new list of verboten words: *trigger warning* is now banned as violent language. So is *picnic*. University of Washington added a few more verboten phrases: *brown bag lunch*, *grandfathered in*, and *blind spot*. Stanford University admins made an even longer one, adding *basket case*. I toured a house, and the real estate agent apologized for accidentally using the term *master bedroom*. Don't even think about using the word *woman*: Johns Hopkins University released a new language guide that defines a *lesbian* as "a non-man attracted to non-men." (Yep, that's me.)

The assertions kept becoming more random and brazen. One I always think about is when a lawyer and frequent MSNBC expert voice made a curious claim: "Rape did not exist among native nations prior to white contact," she wrote. "I repeat, rape *did not exist* among native nations prior to white contact."

Progress itself became suspect. Here's how a top medical journal described a new Alzheimer's drug: "A landmark Alzheimer's drug approval would likely deepen racial inequities in dementia care." Because: "The emergence of any new drug could really widen healthcare disparities that already exist." And when the Covid vaccine meant we could be unmasked, there was *The Washington Post* with the piece: "Masks are off—which means men will start telling women to 'Smile!' again."

The heat was turning up a bit. An NAACP vice president, Michelle Leete, spoke one night at a school rally in Virginia, blasting opponents of the new progressive educational orthodoxy. "Let them die," she said. That seemed a little severe.

The search for skeptics was also growing. A Colorado cake baker once sued over refusing to make a gay wedding cake was sued again for refusing to make a gender-transition cake. Are there no other bakers?

If some of the new rules felt bizarre and maybe oppressive, that was OK. I always think of what one Bay Area business leader wrote: "Effective anti-racism feels like oppression and that's OK. When you're trying to pilot a ship against a current you can't point at the destination."

At the beginning of this, I was covering culture, tech, and power at the *Times*, but I hesitated to write about any of these changes. Not only would this get me in trouble at the paper, but also it was messy for my own moral compass. I owe a lot of my life to political progressivism, and I bristled at the alternative, which certainly wouldn't want me. If you want to be part of the movement for universal health care, which I did and do, then you cannot report critically on #DefundThePolice. If you want to be part of a movement that supports gay marriage, and I did and do, then you can't question whatever disinformation is spread that week. Fine, I can identify as a non-man attracted to non-men. If anything going on in the movement looked anything but perfect, the good reporter knew not to look.

Mind you, I wasn't canceled. Never have been. Nothing hugely dramatic happened to me at the *Times*, really. I suspected my curiosity and my writing would eventually get me in trouble, though, and it did, especially when I talked to people in a few neighborhoods that had indeed abolished their police.

You don't need to hear about how very wounded I was about mean tweets (not that they're seared in my mind, but would you like a list?) or newsroom leaders passing around pictures of me as a teen at a party (fine, I was a debutante). It's a little petty and grimy.

The main group of in-house Narrative Enforcers at the New York Times were the Disinformation Experts, and they clocked me as a problem. One day I was writing a profile of PragerU, a conservative viral-video production studio that had perfected trolling college campuses with funny student-on-the-street videos. After I'd done most of my reporting, I was told that I needed to meet with the in-house Disinformation Expert, a special person who would discuss how to incorporate disinformation analysis into my piece.

I'll call him Todd. He's cool, a prolific Slack presence.

Todd and I chat. He tells me that I need to more fully emphasize the Southern Poverty Law Center assessment of PragerU. The Southern Poverty Law Center started in the 1970s as a civil rights organization filing litigation against the Ku Klux Klan. They've turned now to putting out media reports on everyday conservatives, and their report on PragerU is categorized under "Hatewatch." PragerU is a purveyor of Hate.

The Hatewatch file was based on the work of a sociologist at University of North Carolina at Chapel Hill named Francesca Tripodi. She had "analyzed scriptural inference in conservative news practices," the SPLC explains:

> Tripodi spent extensive time with a conservative women's group and a college Republican group for her study. "It was through these groups that I started learning about PragerU and how much it is a beloved source of news and information amongst most people I spoke with," she tells Hatewatch. "[PragerU] gets people questioning and looking for more information, and if nothing else, it is very blatantly algorithmically connected" to the extreme right content found on YouTube, Tripodi explains.

In other words, this sociologist was accusing PragerU of hate because it was connected, via an algorithm, to other things that were worse.

I needed to chide PragerU for the sin of getting people *questioning* and for the fact that when you search for Republicans on YouTube, you can also eventually find yourself being recommended videos from people further to the right.

I said OK. So I added more SPLC into the story.

In the meantime, I became fascinated by Todd and the movement he was leading inside the paper.

He spent a lot of time in the NYT Slack posting in the #Disinformation channel, which, when I was in it, had some hundred members who posted a stream of conservative news links as a sort of group disinformation watch. Sometimes people would ask about whether something is Bad, like a picture of some people holding three fingers up—Hey, is this white supremacy? (It wasn't.) He'd post TikToks that were apparently disinformation—like a video made by some nurses making fun of Covid restrictions. He'd drop in tweets calling out right-wing internet activity from accounts with names like @socialistdogmom.

Todd was there in Slack to remind everyone that the idea Covid might have come from a lab was a conspiracy theory. He was the authority on these things.

Anyway, this is also not a story about my heroism, pushing back on the disinfo complex. The opposite. In the end, I wanted the hit of that byline. I needed a byline like I needed dinner, and they needed more on PragerU's disinfo.

So I called up someone at Berkeley who I knew would give me the quotes that were needed. And I added to the story:

> Lawrence Rosenthal, chair of the Berkeley Center for Right-Wing Studies, said he notices an impact from PragerU's content, which he describes as close to the edge of conspiratorial disinformation but not quite there.
>
> "It sits at this border between going off a cliff into conspiracy thinking and extreme kinds of prejudices in the name of anti-political correctness," he said.

The piece ran. I got the praise I needed. Good placement too (A1, thank you very much). And I didn't think much more about it.

A few months after the PragerU story, at the height of the frenzied summer of 2020, a large swath of Seattle was taken over as an "autonomous zone." The heart of Seattle's gay neighborhood had been blocked off by masked vigilantes who were maybe throwing a party? As a San Francisco non-man attracted to non-men, I imagined a group taking over the city's gayborhood, The Castro, and declaring it a new city. That seemed kind of fun! But Seattle was turning into chaos, and I knew there were shootings.

All the media I was getting was either extremely right-wing (*look at this woke hellhole*) or very left-wing (*10 reasons why local vigilante violence is actually better than police*). I wanted to get out there and see it. And I found an easy story for a West Coast business reporter: the local businesses were suing the city for encouraging the occupation.

My colleagues sensed something was going wrong when I pitched traveling to Seattle. Why did I want to see what was happening there?

I ran into a colleague who was a rising newsroom leader. He said he was worried about me and this. He was worried about what these story ideas said about me and if I was thinking about my career. He was worried I was into *all this cancel culture stuff.* I said, I'm just so curious about what's going on up there, what else am I supposed to do? He said, "That's a question for a therapist, not an editor."

Antifa was nonsense, fake, a nothing-burger, a non-story, not interesting and not real, he said. The reason he doesn't go to Seattle and cover things like this is because he knows right now is time for white people to sit certain things out. Some things that are not important things shouldn't be covered. The Capitol Hill Autonomous Zone (CHAZ) and whatever was going on there wasn't important. Antifa wasn't important. Why do you care? No but seriously why do you care?

He said when he's old, he always wants to know that he was on the right side of history. Why did I want to be on the wrong side? (I'm pretty sure the extent of my place in history will be in a few family scrapbooks, if I'm very lucky.)

Later, a reporter at *New York* magazine who I knew was friends with my colleagues called me up. He said soberly that he heard I was *red-pilled* and trying to cover things that shouldn't be covered. Did I have any comment?

Finally, there was the issue of my love life. I'd started dating a known liberal dissident on the Opinion side of the paper. A Joe Biden voter who would simply never go Bernie Sanders. A Hillary Clinton voter who never went AOC. She wrote such dissident liberal takes as: "We shouldn't worry so much about 'cultural appropriation' because America thrives when cultures blend," and "The Women's March leaders should stop saying antisemitic things." And we were a couple. We both wanted to write about the movement. We'd fight over whether it was good or bad, me usually arguing the efforts were largely good.

Between dating her and trying to write about the most interesting story of the moment—the revolution!—people very quickly decided I was an in-house enemy. A fascist, right in their midst. The shift was so fast it left me dizzy.

One early evening I was having drinks with an editor and a group of colleagues. The editor, who I liked a lot, heard I was dating this *very bad liberal*. And he looked at me straight in the face and said he thought it was pretty messed up.

He wanted to know: How could I do that? "She's a Nazi. She's a fucking Nazi, Nellie," he said. I tried to laugh it off and he kept going. "Like are you serious, Nellie?" He lobbed another *she's a Nazi*. My colleagues agreed. He kept going. He couldn't believe I would do this, like wow. Eventually I got him to change the subject.

At the time, in the situation at the New York Times, it was normal, or at least becoming so. My colleagues were saying worse. Sometimes quite publicly. Editors who used to chat with me in the cafeteria suddenly pretended I wasn't saying hi. *Maybe California has made me soft?* I wondered, unable to handle standard East Coast media cultural mores. Anyway, I liked that editor. God help me but I still like him. He's a kind man. Other than this. I didn't want to get him in trouble.

He thought my ideas were all a little worse after that.

It feels good to be in the flow of one's community and to be on the side that calls itself justice. And I am in fact for that. I ran the Gay-Straight Alliance at my high school, and I was the only out gay kid for a while, sticking rainbows all around campus. After college, I fit in well with the Brooklyn Left. I've been to a reading of *The Nation* writers at the Verso Books office, and, my God, I bought a tote. When Hillary Clinton was about to win, I was drinking I'm With Her-icanes at a drag bar.

Writing critically about this revolution was placing me outside it, no matter how many disclaimers I put. It didn't matter how I voted or whether technically I shared similar political goals. The only ones who can write about the changes are literal comrades. Otherwise? You're just another fascist pumping out disinformation. As you can imagine, I don't want to be a fascist, and I don't want to produce disinformation.

The trouble is, I became a reporter because I didn't trust authority figures. Newspaper work gave me an opportunity to monetize a suspicious, itchy personality. As a reporter, I spent over a decade working to follow that curiosity. It was hard to suddenly turn that off. It was hard to constantly censor what I was seeing, to close one eye and try *very* hard not to notice anything inconvenient, especially when there was so much to see.

So I started reporting. I don't have any other skills, so that's what I've kept doing here in this book. When I started this, I was a little angry. After I wrote some of these chapters, I quit the paper. And as I continued to report, I married that girlfriend and we started a new media company. It so happened that over the course of these years—dragged out thanks in part to the birth of our daughter—I got to see the arc of the movement as it rose, remaking our institutions from the inside, transforming the country.

I traveled to Portland's late-night Antifa rallies and spent days in the no-cop autonomous zones of Seattle and Minneapolis, looking for utopia. I looked at the attempts to atone for our collective sins, visiting homeless encampments run by BMW-driving socialists and taking courses led by America's leading anti-racist educators, who happen to mostly be middle-aged white women. When the revolution made a turn from race to gender, I followed it, exploring why so many children were being born into the wrong bodies, their genders suddenly so far from their flesh. Finally, I looked back at what we made—reporting on what it all added up to in San Francisco, my hometown. And I looked at what it means to sit out a cancellation. Throughout these chapters, I try to capture the furies of the moment, the hottest battles of a few fiery years.

I want you to see the New Progressive from their own perspective, not as a caricature. Even as I reported on the issues, I was constantly struck by the movement's beauty. There is pleasure and community in cancellation. There's poetry in police abolition.

And some policies are even good. There are statues of historical figures that absolutely should be toppled. There are reparations that should be paid.

The New Progressive is trying to help. They see real problems, real pain. So many of the solutions should work. If only people behaved.

If you've come to this book, maybe you've got your mind set and want to be told how right you are (yes, 2020 was bad, you might say, cracking this open). But my ideal reader for this book, if I'm being honest, is someone like myself, someone who now feels a little tribeless, a person of curiosity, someone whose politics are more exhaustion than doctrine.

This book is also for my family, who are confused about why my beloved old boarding school headmaster released what looked like a hostage video and why there are committees now to propose abandoning Jane Austen and Shakespeare at every prep school in America (but obviously no changes to a $70,000 and up annual tuition—how else would the recording studios stay so lovely?).

This book is for people who want to understand why Abraham Lincoln is canceled and why Lena Dunham is always on the edge. The movement makes new moral rules so fast that "brown-bag lunch" and "trigger warning" are actually bad now. You're probably bad.

When it comes to the rage and indignation, some of it might seem bizarre—how could everyone have been this angry all the time? But I think a lot about allergy science: When the area around a child is very well disinfected, her immune system will keep searching for a fight. It doesn't relax and call it a day. It keeps hunting. It finds peach fuzz and fresh-cut grass, strawberries and pollen. The allergy that develops to those is not fake. The throat tightening and the rash are very real. Broad metrics showing quality of life getting better and more comfortable have nothing to do with what our bodies feel and what they need to do.

So, yes, many Americans are insulated and rich, comfortable and healthy, with plenty of food. It is that rage even during comfort that won me the right to vote and to work and the right to marry a woman and, heck, order sperm online. I know I owe my whole life to the impulse of those who wanted to make what was weird and illegal into what is normal and lauded, to those who saw that things were good but knew they could be better.

But I also know that the immune system looking for new battles can do strange things. It can turn inward and kill its own body.

Part 1

THREE ZONES

A Utopia, If You Can Keep It

It's a little offensive now to say that the occupation of this Seattle neighborhood by a group of anti-fascists was a party, because bad things did happen (a boy was killed), but for a little while, inside the new armed borders of the hippest neighborhood in town, it really was a party.

The neighborhood arose in the summer of 2020, during the surreal months when Covid coincided with the renewed Black Lives Matter movement, which sought to reshape how America polices. White-collar workers were home, Zooming for a meeting or two, freaked out, angry, online, alone, and generally very available, all the time. And America's police were caught on camera doing what sure looked like a murder (a knee held on the neck of a black man). Things felt open-ended and chaotic. When a group of black-clad anti-fascists in ski masks marched into Seattle's historically gay neighborhood of Capitol Hill to start a new police-free autonomous zone, there was a collective shrug. Why not? How about we see?

There'd been protests for a week in the neighborhood before the new borders went up. Police had put barricades around the precinct when the protests heated up, around June 1. Half a dozen elected officials joined in with the anti-fascists and Black Lives Matter crowds to protest. Nights were especially raucous. The crowds grew. Police boarded the precinct windows. They put in stronger barricades. Finally, during the middle of the afternoon of June 8, the police abandoned the precinct. It was a huge win for the protestors. Right away they dragged the police barricades out, using them to build new neighborhood borders. (Eventually Seattle's Department of Transportation would come in to help install nice concrete barriers.) The new city was formed. It was five and a half square blocks.

Along the edges of the community, young men sat on lawn chairs with long guns on their laps. They didn't stop much of anyone, except troublemakers. Reporters, they would sometimes stop. The autonomous zone was not a free-for-all. The young men were mostly locals, public school teachers, baristas, grad students, and various healing arts practitioners. They were masseuses and Reiki specialists. They were vaguely underemployed software engineers working on Zoom. It was less zip-tie-carrying Navy SEALs, like you might find on January 6, and more young people who were described as *sensitive* or stoned. Which is not to say they were uncomfortable with violence. Putting violence back on the table—being armed, being even a little scary—was the core of Antifa's method.

Within the walls of the Capitol Hill Autonomous Zone, the new residents could make a utopia. It would be called CHAZ. It would be a place without the old world's racism and the old ways of talking and thinking. This would be an entirely different project: A fresh start. Anyone who crossed into the new city would be automatically on board. Those who happened to be there already would have to get on board or leave. No one wants to live in capitalist hell—CHAZ was a gift.

The founders of the new neighborhood, set atop the old one, dug into the park lawn and planted a community garden, and the good Seattle mist helped it grow. They set up a free neighborhood library, giving books to all. They set up a clinic providing health care, for everyone, and while the care was basic, it was also free. Food trucks came and musicians did too. Cops couldn't enter CHAZ and didn't need to, thanks to community-run safety efforts and a new culture of equality and compassion that would make crime all but disappear. Weeknights were a smorgasbord of activities—movie nights and dodgeball games, Marxism read-alouds. The city's homeless and addicted were welcomed with open arms. Art could and did go everywhere—on the pavement, the asphalt, the walls of shops and restaurants.

If you didn't know what happened at night and if you didn't look too closely at the armed guards on the edges of the new city, if you didn't see that the community library was just some books on a folding table, and if you didn't think about what exactly was the sewage and waste disposal plan here, if you stopped being so suspicious and just *enjoyed something for once,* then you'd have seen the perfection in CHAZ. For a generation more comfortable tapping on the glass of their phones, here in the newly liberated CHAZ was something tangible.

The neighborhood had been one of those nice, liberal, gentrified ones, with rainbows painted onto the crosswalks. The insurgents who laid claim to those blocks said that progress didn't need to be incremental. It could happen fast. A revolution didn't need to be polite.

Seattle's then mayor, Jenny Durkan, loved it. She was in her early sixties, typically dressed in bright blazers and white pearls, her strawberry blonde hair perfectly blown out into the helmet that's popular for successful women of that age. The autonomous zone had "a block-party atmosphere," she told curious reporters. President Trump took aim at her and the city, describing Seattle as having been taken over by domestic terrorists. He wrote: "Take back your city NOW. If you don't do it, I will. This is not a game. These ugly Anarchists must be stopped IMMEDIATELY. MOVE FAST!" She said instead that it was "a peaceful expression of our community's collective grief and their desire to build a better world." She especially loved the "food trucks, spaghetti potlucks, teach-ins, and movies." She sent barbed wire and Porta-Potties to the autonomous zone.

Politically, lots of anti-fascists are also anarchists, and their goals fit well with many Black Lives Matter activists'. The anti-fascists had been operating in the Pacific Northwest for decades as anti-racist skinheads, a kind of mirror to the more familiar yes-racism skinhead. These proto-Antifas went by the moniker Skinheads Against Racial Prejudice, or SHARP. Meanwhile, Black Lives Matter, a social-media-hashtag-turned-protest-movement started in the 2010s, had grown, primarily thanks to the warm embrace from glossy magazines and CEOs. Antifa wants the destruction of capitalism and the state's monopoly on violence, while BLM wants a deep expansion of state power and potentially a new national anti-racism branch. So there were some differences.

But both groups hated the cops. Both groups wanted the abolition of police and prisons. The chant—"No good cops in a racist system"—worked for both of them. BLM's corporate consultants needed a military arm, so they could work together for a little while.

There was a list of demands for the return of the neighborhood to the City of Seattle. They included abolition of imprisonment, along with *de-gentrification* and more equitable history lessons for elementary school children.

CHAZ leaders wanted autonomy, and they got it. They were free. The police were told not to enter these blocks. Signs hung at the border: *No good cops no bad protestors* and *No cops no problem*. They would create a localized anti-crime system. The anti-fascists were pulling off their ski masks, and everyone was getting along. Seattle was going all in.

It's hard to tell when exactly CHAZ turned dark. Any troubles in the zone were downplayed. But online, shaky and dimly lit videos of CHAZ at night depicted big men passing out guns.

Groups seemed to be doling out punishments, shoving people, screaming, shooting. But the videos were hard to interpret. And the only places that posted them were right-wing websites that pumped them out with blaring all-caps headlines. It was all SEATTLE DESTROYED BY LIBERALS. I didn't trust any of it. So I got on a plane and flew to Seattle.

Faizel Khan, who watched the barricades grow stronger through the windows of his café, wasn't opposed to the occupation per se. A gay man, he had moved from Texas to Seattle's Capitol Hill to be somewhere welcoming and fun. He wanted a less racist country and believed in Black Lives Matter.

He called his shop Cafe Argento. Their tagline on Facebook: *12th Avenue's Sexiest Coffee House.* They made a great egg sandwich. For a while, things in his new city seemed alright. He supported Black Lives Matter because he supported progress.

His new city officials—that loose collective of anti-fascists and local Black Lives Matter leaders—held meetings to announce the community events. It was unclear how leadership of their new city was structured, who exactly was making decisions. But people were coming in from all over to see the new city, and for a little while the businesses were OK. It didn't last.

When I met Faizel in July 2020, he was outside his café having a cigarette. I'd read his name in a lawsuit. Faizel and other small business owners and local residents were suing the city and the mayor. The city had abandoned business owners, the lawsuit asserted, and the mayor was aiding and abetting the insurgents. That city officials marched with the protestors and that the city helped build the barriers and provided Porta-Potties was bad, but also the city had stopped police and emergency services to the region. No fire trucks, no ambulances.

The lovely gay neighborhood might have been police-free but there was definitely policing. Half a dozen security teams wandered around the neighborhood, armed with handguns and rifles, open and concealed. Some of the teams wore official-looking private security uniforms. These were newly hired by local businesses and condos.

Others wore casual clothes and lanyards identifying their affiliation with Black Lives Matter. These were BLM security, typically longtime activists and locals. There were socialist gun rights fans, like members of the Puget Sound John Brown Gun Club, cruising through performing security services.

Another armed group wore all black with no identifying labels and declined to name their group affiliation when I asked. This group was rangier, stranger looking, mostly white. Faizel called CHAZ "a white occupation," and this group definitely seemed in charge.

I stayed near Faizel for a while, hearing stories as his friends stopped by to describe the bizarre details of life under occupation in a great American city—a group of liberal gays and local Seattle shopkeeps who became the embodiment of fascism.

There was Matthew Ploszaj, who lives a few blocks from the café, who said his apartment building was broken into four times during the occupation. The Seattle police were called each time and never came to his apartment, he said.

There were the employees of Bergman's Lock and Key, who said they were followed by demonstrators with baseball bats. Cure Cocktail, a local bar and charcuterie, said its workers were asked by protesters to pledge loyalty to CHAZ: "Are you for the CHAZ or are you for the police?" Bill Donner, the owner of Richmark Label, made the mistake of letting police officers use the roof of his factory to monitor the occupation one day. His company had spent fifty years making labels for products like whiskey, soaps, and natural beef jerky. During the occupation, Bill had to negotiate with the occupiers of the zone for access to his factory. Twice, he called 911 and was told that the police would not be coming into the area.

There was John McDermott. His shop was right across from Faizel's.

It's a funky old auto repair shop called Car Tender. One night, John was driving his wife home from their anniversary dinner when he got a call from a neighbor who saw someone trying to break into his shop. John and his twenty-seven-year-old son, Mason, raced over. A man who was inside the shop, John said, had emptied the cash drawer and was in the midst of setting the building on fire. John said he and his son wrestled the man down and planned to hold him until the police arrived. Officers didn't show up. A group of several hundred protesters did, breaking down the chain-link fence around his shop and claiming that John had kidnapped the man. His voice cracked when he told me about it. "They started coming across the fence—you see all these beautiful kids, a mob but kids—and they have guns and

10

are pointing them at you and telling you they're going to kill you. Telling me I'm the KKK," he said. "I'm not the KKK."

The demonstrators were live-streaming the confrontation. John's wife watched, frantically calling anyone she could think of to go help him. Later, John's photo and shop address appeared on a website called Cop Blaster, whose stated aim is to track police brutality but also has galleries of what it calls "Snitches" and "Cop Callers." The McDermotts, alongside many others, were categorized as both on the website, which warned they should "keep their mouths shut."

Since the Cop Blaster post went up, John's shop received harassing phone calls and messages. Some employees took time off.

As I talked to Faizel and his neighbors, a tall man in a trench coat and hiking boots walked over. He spread his coat open casually, showing several pistols on harnesses around his chest and waist. Faizel and I quieted. For a second I was scared, but then he gave a big smile.

He presented a badge on a lanyard that read "Black Lives Matter Community Patrol."

His name is Rick Hearns and he identified himself as a longtime security guard and mover who is now a Black Lives Matter community guard, in charge of several other guards. Local merchants pay for his protection, he said as he handed out his business card to all of us.

Things had gotten out of hand, he said. He blamed the destruction and looting on "opportunists," but also said that much of the damage on Capitol Hill came from a distinct contingent of violent, armed activists. "It's Antifa," he said. "They don't want to see the progress we've made."

Pretty much anyone with enough money to do so decided to leave Capitol Hill, to wait out the occupation. But Faizel stayed.

Café sales plummeted. Very few people braved the barricades set up by the armed occupiers to come in for his coffee and breakfast sandwiches. Cars coming to pick up delivery orders would turn around.

Twice, Faizel and his workers were so scared they called 911. Both times police refused to enter. They said he could meet them a few blocks away, if they really needed help.

Faizel watched as encampments took over the sidewalks. He saw roving bands of masked protesters smashing windows and looting at night. That force of young men, nearly all of them white, created a heavily armed border right by his shop. To get in now, he would have to ask permission of these new guards.

"They barricaded us all in here," he said. "And they were sitting in lawn chairs with guns."

Most businesses got on board fast. Like Molly Moon's Homemade Ice Cream, whose owner posted about how "beautiful" and "peaceful" the autonomous zone was.

The new leadership identified Faizel as one of the business owners who was *not on board* and they sat outside his café with those rifles and tormented customers who tried to walk in. The café windows were shattered one night, and the place was trashed. Many days Faizel worked pulling espressos in the dark, his windowpanes filled with large sheets of plywood.

CHAZ didn't close after nineteen-year-old Horace Lorenzo

Anderson Jr. was shot in its borders. The shooting happened after hours, when the tourists and families and friendly reporters had tucked back into their homes in nice neighborhoods of the very lovely city. The people who had stayed overnight were the activists, the anti-racist skinheads, the BLM die hards. Volunteer "medics" treated Anderson inside of CHAZ. Seattle's paramedics could not enter without police escort. Lorenzo's father said in a lawsuit that Anderson was put on a makeshift medical table, where he simply bled to death.

Eventually, CHAZ residents put him into the back of a pickup truck and drove him to Harborview Medical Center. The City of Seattle agreed to pay $500,000 in the wrongful-death suit. Surveillance video actually captured the shooting, and police charged the killer within weeks, but he wasn't arrested for a year.

After Lorenzo was murdered, CHAZ stayed open. Things were bad but maybe that's what we all deserved. The world before CHAZ was maybe worse (it's hard to remember).

Three more people were shot within and around CHAZ, and still it stayed open.

The second teenager to die was what finally ended the occupation.

No one ever figured out who killed sixteen-year-old Antonio Mays Jr. and injured the fourteen-year-old next to him as they drove a white Jeep in CHAZ. As I said, ambulances weren't allowed into the zone, so one victim was put into someone's car, another was carried out to the edge of the zone and put into an ambulance there.

By the time police entered, five hours later, the car and scene had been cleared of evidence, police said. Mays died. No one was ever charged with the shooting.

As the violence turned deadly, Kshama Sawant, who was at the time in Seattle's city council, representing the Capitol Hill neighborhood and a member of the Socialist Alternative party, defended the protesters' use of their own armed guards instead of the police.

"Elected committees of self defense have historically played vital roles during general strikes, occupations, and in mass movements, in order for the working class and marginalized people to defend themselves and carry out necessary functions in place of the forces of the state," she wrote in June of that summer. She has called for the local police precinct to be permanently placed under "community control."

The occupation lasted less than a month altogether. Seattle's mayor sent in police officers to end it, and Kshama wrote on Twitter, "Shame on Mayor Jenny Durkan for deploying Seattle police yesterday in a brutal attack against peaceful Black Lives Matter protesters & homeless neighbors at the Capitol Hill Organized Protest."

The borders to CHAZ came down. The whole thing was coming apart and getting patched back together. Big guys in orange vests were hoisting new glass panes into windows. Other groups were spraying down the sidewalks, sweating, and scrubbing off graffiti and the urine. Shattered streetlamps were being unscrewed and replaced.

The CHAZ loyalists had moved to a small park, where they

set up tents and waited to retake the space. They were mostly smoking pot, waiting for night. They wore all black and had the innocuous-looking accessories I would grow accustomed to: umbrellas to block my camera, cans of soup to hurl, skateboards to shove, black motorcycle helmets fitted with GoPros to capture the moment someone shoved back, a few seconds that would be spliced and streamed.

They didn't want to make friends, but they saw my notebook and saw me talking to people. They wanted me to know they knew I was there, so I usually felt one of those unnamed black-clad people watching me. Weeks later, crowded in a dark park in Portland, reading one of my stories about the movement aloud to rally themselves into rage before going out to march the streets, they would scream my name. But in Seattle we were all still strangers.

They were not just white but had the very pale skin of the always overcast Pacific Northwest. They were in their teens and early twenties, with that coiled squirrely energy men have then. Most of the boys in the park that day were open-carrying semi-automatic rifles across their backs or wore pistols on their chests. Some had knives in holsters around their calves.

Every now and then, the group gathered and someone would give a speech on a bullhorn about the importance of disbanding the police. Sometimes the activists stood up and reflected about what went wrong with the occupation, shouting it into the group or onto the sidewalk.

One young woman on a bullhorn argued to anyone who would listen that the problem was only that police left too quickly and that a sustainable police-free region would have to be built more slowly: "What did they think would happen?"

When CHAZ was finally cleared in July of 2020, curiously, so were Mayor Jenny Durkan's text messages from the period. And those of the chief of police. And the fire chief. Thousands of them. The city agreed to settle a lawsuit for $200,000, promising to be better at record retention the next time they let someone seize a neighborhood of the city.

Faizel repaired the shop again and again with new sheets of glass. Eventually, it all got too hectic for him. He came to Seattle to enjoy his life, not to take part in a daily battle. Eventually, he dropped out of the lawsuit against the city. He just wanted to be left alone. He said he didn't want to talk about those months. Business was finally coming back. People were finally forgetting about the seasons when Faizel Khan at his espresso maker was the closest enemy anti-fascists could find.

And quietly, almost exactly three years after the neighborhood was first taken over and renamed CHAZ, the ice cream shop owner Molly Moon Neitzel filed a lawsuit against the city. She wanted to be really clear that she still supports the police-free utopia. But also the city needs to pay her for having abolished the police in the police-free utopia. "This lawsuit does not seek to undermine [CHAZ] participants' message or present a counter message," her lawyers write. "Rather, this lawsuit is about Plaintiff's constitutional and other legal rights of which were overrun by the City of Seattle's decision to abandon and close off an entire city neighborhood, leaving it unchecked by the police."

Masked Vigilantes Have Always Saved the World

Taking over and losing Seattle's gayborhood was a mess but it was too small, anyway. Who needed all those whining coffee-shop neoliberals? The important thing was that the Black Lives Matter activists and Antifa had found each other.

It was a summer of rage, and cities around the country were seeing rallies. People, still stuck at home, still masked from the pandemic, were taking to the streets at night. Shops were getting torched for racial justice but also because it just feels good to burn something down sometimes. Portland was a crucial nexus for the protest organizers.

One night, there were overlapping events promoted on Portland's Black Lives Matter Events page: The official "nonviolent protest" in the city center. This was the Black Lives Matter official protest. Then there was "an autonomously organized direct action march protesting systemic racism & police brutality."

I went to both. First, the nonviolent one. But no one showed up, except local news and a dozen police officers milling around. Much was made about how BLM and the harder-edged Antifa were *super separate things*, but it almost seemed like the BLM event had been posted knowing it was fake. There weren't two separate events at all because there was only one protest.

So I drove out to the "direct action" event. It was in an unlit park in a residential neighborhood, and people started gathering around 8 p.m. Everyone wore black. Many of the protestors had on body armor and motorcycle helmets. They hung out in the park, talking quietly, until it was completely dark.

Then suddenly, a group of people arrived. Moving quickly, they created a little village. Many of these new organizers were middle-aged women wearing colorful clothes and university-branded lanyards. They opened folding tables and supply booths. The attendees used cell phones for light to study the goods. I joined in, looking around.

There was a food table overflowing with protein bars and Monster energy drinks. There was new body armor, motorcycle helmets right out of the box, shields and umbrellas, all free.

The young protestors were getting geared up in the dark. The energy was something like a carnival.

"Paint balloons, get your paint balloons," someone barked. "Paint balloons!"

A small free literature selection was set up on the grass and overseen by three people in ski masks. They nodded hello. It was a popular offering, and people crowded around, craning to see the pamphlets.

Titles included "Why We Break Windows," "In Defense of Smashing Cameras," and "Three-Way Fight: Revolutionary Anti-Fascism and Armed Self-Defense."

Around 9:30, the group was in some organizational chaos. They had decided that the neighborhood close by was too racially diverse for them to protest in. They needed to go somewhere whiter.

So the protesters caravanned twenty minutes away to Alberta, a more affluent neighborhood that began being gentrified in the 1990s. They reassembled and marched through the streets. Neighbors in impressive Craftsman-style homes pulled down their shades and turned off their lights. Many could be seen peering out of dark windows.

We moved as a large group through the middle of the road. We were almost entirely white, but at the front, a young black person of ambiguous gender presentation twerked and periodically screamed.

One woman stepped out of an expansive home looking angry; upon seeing the crowd, she quickly retreated indoors. A few young couples stood in their doorways. A black woman driving past honked and cheered. One white man stepped onto his patio clapping and hollering in support of the passing march. The group called for him to join. He smiled and waved them on, still clapping. They began to chant that he was spineless. He looked worried. Eventually the march moved along, and he went back into his house. "You'll never sleep tight, we do this every night," the protesters chanted.

This was a time when the mainstream media toyed with the idea that righteous vigilantes were good, very good. And only the weak-kneed would question whether the protest should have a little edge, that frisson of danger. People's hearts are always in the right place.

The protest was fiery but peaceful, is how a now-famous CNN chyron described one Antifa outing. The correspondent was reporting against a backdrop of raging fires as the word *peaceful* sat on the screen. The scene looked comically unpeaceful. "We don't have time to finger-wag at protestors about property," said Black Lives Matter cofounder Alicia Garza.

Ignoring destruction of a local business became official policy for New York–based media. David Remnick, the editor of *The New Yorker*, wrote a meditation at the height of the protests, asking, "Who, really, is the agitator here?" He cites Martin Luther King Jr.: "Even looting, [King] insisted, is an act of catharsis, a form of 'shocking' the white community 'by abusing property rights.' Then King quoted Victor Hugo to deepen his point: 'If a soul is left in the darkness, sins will be committed. The guilty one is not he who commits the sin, but he who causes the darkness.'" That's the kicker to Remnick's essay.

NPR held a friendly Q and A about the importance of riots and looting as a protest tactic with the author of a book titled simply "In Defense of Looting."

Nikole Hannah-Jones, the creator of The 1619 Project and by then the most famous American reporter, agreed: "Violence is when an agent of the state kneels on a man's neck until all of the life is leached out of his body. Destroying property, which can be replaced, is not violence. To use the same language to describe those two things is not moral," she told CBS News.

Anyway, Antifa itself was just fun! *Masked vigilantes have always saved the world* became the media's line.

Another prominent reporter for the *Times* tweeted: "If your grandfather fought in the war against Nazi Germany or Imperial Japan, they were antifa."

Writer and director W. Kamau Bell did a special on Antifa for CNN. "Antifa is short for anti-fascist," he said. "Picture a table: On one side of the table is Hitler and Mussolini, and on the other side is the popular performer Raffi. Which side of the table you sitting on? I'm with Raffi."

In a video called "The Real Antifa," The Lincoln Project, a lobbying group for Democrats spearheaded by former Republicans, showed clips of World War II soldiers while a gravelly-voiced narrator read: "Anti-fascism. It's not a cable news talking point, it's an American ideal that should be memorialized."

Or perhaps another way of putting it: "Loot and burn everything. Fuck this. Who the fuck cares about looting????" wrote Imani Gandy, an editor with the progressive Rewire News Group. "Stop killing us."

Maybe destroying small business was good. Small businesses aren't unionized. Small businesses aren't accountable. All those little burned-out shops were part of the structural problem. Bhaskar Sunkara, president of *The Nation*, a major leftist magazine, said essentially that it was bad tactics but good politics to end small businesses: "So if [by] 'attack small businesses' you mean encouraging the looting of them, sure, that's tactically counterproductive. But we should aim to undermine small business owners with pro-worker legislation/unions and to reconstitute them as worker-controlled state firms or coops." A writer for the progressive magazine *Jacobin* joined in: "We shouldn't fetishize mom and pops. They offer lower wages, skimpier benefits, and inferior labor protections."

Delighted by the warm press reception, random members of Antifa started releasing their own statements and appearing on news shows, their faces backlit to keep anonymity: "The use of violence is a tactic of how we keep our communities safe," an anonymous member told *Nightline*.

"The whole point of protesting is to make people uncomfortable," said Congresswoman Alexandria Ocasio-Cortez.

A *Slate* magazine headline read: "Non-violence is an important tool for protests, but so is violence."

The rhetoric of the time was, at best, heated, even occasionally exceeding the ever-polite Trump. One prominent activist and media darling tweeted at Florida governor Ron DeSantis: "I am going to be the person who watches the life leave your eyes."

Jerry Taylor, the former president of the Niskanen Center, a mainstream liberal think tank, wrote about how he would murder the two Saint Louis homeowners who brandished guns when protestors marched down their street to protest at the mayor's house.

"If I were in that march, and these racist lunatics were waving guns at me, I'd like to think I'd rush them and beat their brains in," Jerry wrote. "And I wouldn't apologize for it for one goddam second."

Antifa had its own press and literature anyway. The pamphlets I picked up in Portland were low-tech, printed in black and white, stapled together. They were meant to be distributed freely and often, you would see them anywhere you went.

Compared to the rhetoric of the Black Lives Matter folks, which tended toward the *in this house we believe* . . . mode, the Antifa literature was direct. I picked up a pamphlet with the subtle title *I Want to Kill Cops Until I'm Dead*. It goes:

Police Officers must be killed, the families of Police Officers must be killed, the children of Police Officers must be killed, the friends and supporters of Police Officers must be killed. We mean this both materially and immaterially (though both meanings do not necessarily apply to all of the above examples); in undoing the murderous reign of terror inflicted upon us by the guardians of 'civilization,' it is required not only to wipe them from the face of the earth; but further that we act in such extremity that the reemergence of any 'police style' force inside the reality proceeding

23

policing's annihilation is not only discouraged, but is in fact impossible.

We will not address, nor entertain questions of morality here, whether murder is right or wrong, whether or not the children of Police Officers deserve to die, whether we will be able to live with ourselves after the rivers of blood. . . .

We want to expand the definition of police to include doctors, midwives, and psychologists who violently police gender and sexuality at the point of birth.

Toward the end, acknowledging that the bloody battle has to start somewhere, they offer three "pretty easy" ways to damage police forces.

First: "Our favorite simple timed device to burn a cop car is an ethanol jelly stove." Then: "Removing a small amount of air from tires in the hope of enabling a car crash." And last: "Partly severing a vehicle's brake cables."

A brochure called "Piece Now; Peace Later" bills itself as an anarchist's guide to firearms, with an emphasis on carry laws, safety, and field stripping and cleaning. "The reason for beginning to share firearm skills now is that the ability to conduct successful armed actions, even on a small-scale, does not emerge overnight."

This zine could be some traditional gun-nut material, except that it focuses on the history of slavery and includes a bit more on the problematic gender dynamics in anarchist gun ownership: "Most of the gun-owning anarchists we know are men, and it is readily apparent that it will take a tremendous amount of work, on both men and women's part, to make basic firearms skills accessible beyond the manarchist milieu."

The booklet recommends the AK-47, which is what I saw most of the Antifa carrying in Seattle: "That weapon is so affordable, reliable, available, and easy to use."

The cost of protests kept adding up. One community relief fund in Minneapolis, where early protests included vandalism and arson, raised millions for businesses along the Lake Street corridor, a largely Latino and East African business district.

Allison Sharkey, the executive director of the Lake Street Council, which was organizing the fund, told me: "We asked the small businesses what they needed to cover the damage that insurance wasn't paying, and the gap was around $200 million."

Her own office, between a crafts market and a Native American support center, was burned down in the protests. Some small businesses resorted to posting GoFundMe pleas for donations online, though others are nervous about speaking out lest they lend ammunition to a conservative critique of the Black Lives Matter movement.

In Portland, Elizabeth Snow McDougall, the owner of Stevens-Ness Law Publishing Co., emphasized her support for the cause before describing the damage done to her business.

"One window broken, then another, then another, then another. Garbage to clean off the sidewalk in front of the store every morning. Urine to wash out of our doorway alcove. Graffiti to remove. Costs to board up—and later we'll have costs to repair."

Protestors became more confrontational with other people as the summer went on. They surrounded a diner in Washington, DC, who refused to raise her fist to show support for Black Lives Matter. She didn't have a political feeling against the movement—she just didn't like the pressure. They circled her, screaming.

In Rochester, New York, protesters would surround people at outdoor restaurants and chant at them and shake their dinner tables.

They surrounded a random taqueria in New York City for a while one night, yelling, "Get the fuck out of New York" and screaming that white-owned taquerias aren't welcome here. It helped that during the pandemic, everyone out that night was eating outside, and so diners were quite accessible.

One night in mid-2021, I was having dinner in the West Village. A group of protestors passed by, chanting at outdoor diners someone had *got to go* . . . I started chatting with a young white protestor who asked me to pledge that I also wanted the police commissioner fired. She didn't want me to sign anything or give money but just to agree that he should be fired. Sure!

Despite the support from local mayors and elite coastal media, Antifa couldn't keep their momentum. Seattle fell apart with the murders; other autonomous zones kept combusting wherever they tried them, and the larger coalition was a mess. The sheen was wearing off, the violence losing some of its excitement. And that was a problem. Black Lives Matter had to clean up. Black Lives Matter was getting major funding. Black Lives Matter was going much more mainstream. Mug shots of wild-eyed young anti-fascists with gauge earrings and half-shaved heads were not the vibe anymore. Donor funds still paid to bail them out, of course, over and over. But Black Lives Matter was moving on.

Abolitionist Entertainment LLC

Everyone had wanted to do *something* to join in as the protest movement grew into 2021. Everyone wanted to help. Everyone wanted to give. Maybe it was just posting a black square on Instagram to show solidarity, but often it was more. Friends started sending money and organizing others to do the same. I'd get a barrage of Instagram Stories posts from old classmates encouraging everyone to give to Black Lives Matter and various maybe-related nonprofits—"support Shaun King" was a frequent ask. (The journalist and activist Shaun King is either a longtime skimmer of social justice fundraising or the victim of a prolonged and aggressive campaign by dozens of people to undermine him, whichever seems more likely.) I started giving to a few new groups myself.

The organizations that already existed in places like Minneapolis and the new organizations that sprang up to capture this energy were flooded with volunteers and, most importantly, cash. People marched and people gave. Corporate America did too. And they all kept giving.

The Washington Post estimates $50 billion was promised between mid-2020 and mid-2021. Lots of that money came from corporate donations and megafunders like George Soros, who dropped $220 million into fancy nonprofits that sprang up like mushrooms—but also everyday people were sending in small donations. A lot of them.

Despite all the noise nationally, in March 2021, when the police officer accused of murdering Floyd went on trial, it was surprisingly quiet in Minneapolis, where I went to cover things. The flashiest new organizations with the best names and sharpest websites were hard to find. They were not at the courthouse. They could not meet me for coffee or a drink or a walk or even a Zoom. They weren't hosting anything in town that week. None of their representatives seemed to be in Minneapolis at all.

The more I walked around in Minneapolis and talked to the earlier generation of activists, the stranger it seemed. No one in Minneapolis seemed to know where all the money had gone.

Over at the courthouse, there were half a dozen protestors the morning the trial started. They were milling around having granola bars and when the police would ask them, again, to please not erect sunshade tents, then they would chant *No good cops in a racist system*. One person called a black cop a "house [n-word]."

One protestor chained herself to the fence. I sidled up next to her. White volunteer guards watched me warily and took notes—"We're protecting our community," they told me.

It was a jarring image: a black woman with chains, heavy and thick, locked around her. But she was also happy and very friendly.

Her name is Samantha and she supports abolishing the police.

"You can't reform a racist system," she said. "The police were created literally to be a slave patrol. You cannot reform that."

She said she was annoyed by how many activists in Minneapolis these days were being paid by a violence prevention program to be out on the streets.

Samantha said she wasn't being paid. She did have, however, a corporate diversity consulting firm she wanted to tell me and the other folks about. She would have given us her card but . . . , she said with a laugh and a wiggle of her chains, she didn't have a free hand.

One morning during the opening week of the trial, a group of longtime activists gathered at a hotel. Their nonprofits have basic websites; the snacks are Cheetos and M&Ms. They had come together here near city hall to brainstorm on the latest piece of police reform legislation they were hoping to push through.

Their demands were being debated by the state senate that day, and so far it wasn't going well.

At the meeting were a few people, including an older woman, Michelle Gross, a retired nurse and longtime activist who runs Communities United Against Police Brutality. Also there was Johnathon McClellan, the founder and president of the Minnesota Justice Coalition and a retired firefighter, now in law school. Also there is the mother of a young man who had died in a county jail.

"He walked into jail healthy, and nine days later they carried him out in a body bag," said Del Shea Perry. Her son, Hardel Sherrell, was twenty-seven when he died in a Minnesota jail. "They didn't want to hear him crying in jail, so they gotta hear his mom now."

In the world of police accountability activism, they're relatively old-timers. They want moderate reforms. They want more accountability from the police. And they want a specialized mental health division to be the first responders for 911 calls that involve nonviolent mental health issues. If someone, let's say, has mental illness, Michelle believes police should not be the first responders.

"Every county in the state already has a mobile crisis response team, and yet our 911 call centers don't refer calls to them," Michelle explains.

Despite national attention to the problems the local activists are addressing, their efforts are struggling. That day they were frustrated.

"'Abolish the police' ruined us," someone said.

"The Abolish the Police movement, it confused the issue. It made it challenging," said Johnathon. "It made it challenging for us to push legislation. The Abolish the Police movement was used to draw a line in the sand. We had a lot of legislative initiatives, but then we had to keep explaining how our policies were different from abolish."

The abolish activists—a coalition that called itself Yes 4 Minneapolis—put together a charter amendment, intended to go on the ballot in late 2021, to replace its police department with a Department of Public Safety. Fighting together for this was a clutch of cool, flashy nonprofits—Black Visions Collective, Reclaim the Block, and TakeAction Minnesota. Yes 4 Minneapolis became the effort that seized online attention. Abolish the Minneapolis police department! It was backed by the heavies in this world like the American Civil Liberties Union, and it reported raising about a million dollars for the fight. Meanwhile, the commonsense reform efforts of the local activists were losing ground.

"You know what we call TakeAction? Fake Action," said Michelle. "You have Yes 4 Minnesota promoting this fake charter." She's shaking her head. "They're talking about getting rid of the police but not what will replace it."

"By putting up posters with their little QR code in George Floyd Square, this group raised $30 million," Michelle said. "All they're doing is promoting a poorly written, illegal charter amendment. It makes it even harder to hold police accountable, did you know that? And we're like, 'Why are you pushing this?' We know that the community does not even want it. It's crap. It's a giant distraction. It's utterly ridiculous."

Another longtime activist, DJ Hooker, who organizes with Twin Cities Coalition for Justice 4 Jamar, was pushing for people to investigate the groups. A bunch of local nonprofits are demanding the attorney general look into these newer nonprofits. An open letter demanding answers was published: Who are you? How much have you raised? Where is it going? Locals had never heard of these groups before, and suddenly they were the face of Minneapolis and justice, the letter said.

"You never see them. You never hear from them. The Soros money and stuff like that, they don't do protests and talk to people in the community. They're spending it on very high salaries to do—we're not quite sure! We can't really figure out what they're doing with the money. They really don't communicate with any of the activists," Hooker said.

Johnathon told me he can't understand why reporters keep coming to town and quoting representatives from what he sees as fake nonprofits. He can't understand why no one wants to cover the corruption.

"We think over $600 million flowed into the big organizations doing justice work in Minneapolis," Johnathon said.

"It's theft. It's theft," he said. "What happened here is theft."

That November, the police abolition charter initiative those trendy groups were pushing was thoroughly defeated by voters.

Then something interesting happened. Since then, since the

attention and radical chic moved elsewhere, the incrementalists have had a bunch of wins. In late June 2021, they got Travis' Law passed, which requires 911 call centers to send mental health crisis teams for mental health crisis calls. In 2022, they got deep restrictions put on no-knock warrants. And Del Shea Perry? She got the Hardel Sherrell Act passed. It sets standards around medical care and establishes more state oversight over county jails.

"The guy that was running Reclaim the Block, I think he moved out of town," Michelle said, citing one of the police abolition nonprofits. "Or at least, we've never seen him again. We don't know who the hell they are. Black Visions Collective, we've never seen 'em again."

Black Visions Collective and Reclaim the Block raised more than $30 million in the aftermath of George Floyd.

I look up Black Visions one day in late 2023.

Their website now reads: "We are nearing the end of a multi-year strategic planning process in which we have been discerning the future goals, structures, relationships, and accountability needed for Black Visions to thrive. During this time of reflection, we have decided to pause much of our external programming and community organizing." Reclaim the Block's most recent post is an announcement about wrapping up operations: "Our Sunset: December, 2023."

Del Shea Perry wasn't the only parent who was wondering where the money was going. Samaria Rice, the mother of Tamir

Rice, a twelve-year-old killed by police in 2014, joined with another mother of a black child killed by police. In spring 2021 she wrote an open letter to the Black Lives Matter Global Network.

"We don't want or need y'all parading in the streets accumulating donations, platforms, movie deals, etc. off the death of our loved ones, while the families and communities are left clueless and broken," they wrote. "Don't say our loved ones' names period! That's our truth!"

Michael Brown Sr., whose eighteen-year-old son Michael Brown was killed in Ferguson, Missouri, setting off an infamous series of protests, said he and the activists in his community haven't seen a penny.

"Who are they giving the money to, and what are they doing with it?" he said in a video, asking for money for the Ferguson community. "Why hasn't my family's foundation received any assistance from the movement? How could you leave the families who are helping the community without any funding?"

The Black Lives Matter Global Network is the largest and most well-funded nationwide entity using the name Black Lives Matter. Begun in 2013 after the killing of Trayvon Martin, it aggressively escalated fundraising as the protests of 2020 rocked the country. It raised nearly $100 million that year alone.

A typical email from BLM Global Network:

Invest in the community: Donate to the George Floyd Memorial Foundation as we honor George Floyd's legacy by uniting and activating our communities to challenge the root causes of racial inequity and end the systemic violence affecting Black Americans.

And then, the email subject line: [SHOP NOW] Shop BLM's Fall collection >>

Michael Brown Sr. got some answers as more people began to demand transparency. The organization and others like it were compelled to open the books, file IRS reports, and answer questions. Sometimes.

Sometimes the activities of leaders in this arena were disclosed. That's how we found out that Patrisse Khan-Cullors, the cofounder of the organization, who bills herself as a "trained Marxist" and as the woman who invented the #BlackLivesMatter hashtag, had just bought a $1.4 million home in the tony hills of Topanga Canyon, California. She bought it under an LLC called Abolitionist Entertainment.

Actually, she'd bought four homes in a few years, including one in Georgia with its own plane hangar, all told worth nearly $3 million. (Her earlier homes were more modest, like a $590,000 house she'd bought in South Los Angeles in 2018.) She'd been eyeing a luxury apartment on a private resort in the Bahamas where the cheapest homes are $5 million, the *New York Post* said. (In a twist that reflected the current moment's mode, the first *New York Post* story detailing Patrisse's real-estate empire was blocked from being shared on Facebook, because it "violated community standards.")

She'd been having fun. Her group Reform LA Jails had a $26,000 bill at a luxury Malibu beach resort, then a "summit +

day party" in Pasadena, then hosted a party at Jane Fonda's house.

She had a CAA agent, a multiyear deal with Warner Bros. Television Group, and a bestselling memoir. But Black Lives Matter said they hadn't paid her very much money over the years, just $120,000 in consulting fees—though they did in 2020 pay more than $800,000 to a company owned by her brother for security services. (Plus $969,459 to a company owned by the father of her child to "produce live events" and provide other "creative services.") Black Lives Matter Global Network Foundation issued a statement about the criticism, calling it racism to question how or why she bought her houses.

"It continues a tradition of terror by white supremacists against Black activists," Patrisse said. "The way that I live my life is in direct support to Black people, including my Black family members, first and foremost," she later explained to *Black News Tonight* reporter Marc Lamont Hill.

She stepped down from Black Lives Matter anyway.

Eventually, the Black Lives Matter movement spending got so egregious it turned, for me personally, aspirational. Black Lives Matter gave enough money to a nonprofit run by Patrisse's former spouse, Janaya Khan, to buy a 10,000-square-foot mansion—the former headquarters of the Communist Party—in Toronto for $6.3 million. The city put in another $250,000 for renovations.

They're calling it the Wildseed Centre for Art & Activism and the tagline is "make the revolution irresistible," a quote from the black author Toni Cade Bambara. How do you make it irresistible? Make it a party. As the center described itself from the start:

The Wildseed Centre for Art & Activism is a transfeminist queer affirming brick-and-mortar space that serves to nurture radical Black creation. It was birthed by BLM-Canada artists and activists who recognized the need for enduring space to cultivate the creative grounds of Toronto's diverse Black communities.

But there were very few public events listed at Wildseed. There was a web page for booking the space, but actually no one was allowed to book the space—Covid precautions. There was a page called "Access" but it was just about actual access: "Wildseed Centre is an accessible venue in downtown T'karón:to. There is a ramp to the door."

It later turned out that in October 2020, BLM had made another purchase that they didn't want to tell anyone about. They called it "Campus," and they wanted to use it as an "influencer house" or maybe for security of its leadership, though clearly it couldn't be both. Campus cost $5.88 million, and it's a 7,400-square-foot "Farm House Style Compound" with 7 bedrooms and 6.5 baths, 24 parking spaces, and a 2,300-square-foot soundstage. Very Los Angeles.

Patrisse Cullors's mother was hired as a cleaner, even as Patrisse began a YouTube cooking show in the expansive kitchen. They called the holding company used to buy the house 3726 Laurel Canyon LLC, an address that can be shared because it was bought with tax-deductible charitable donations.

When the news of the new house broke—it was reported by a black investigative reporter named Sean Campbell, an adjunct assistant professor at the Columbia Graduate School of Journalism—Patrisse called it a "despicable abuse of a platform." She added: "Journalism is supposed to mitigate harm and inform our communities."

During an event at the Vashon Center for the Arts, a venue on a gorgeous, very white island off the coast of Seattle, Patrisse spoke about the organization's financial chaos and urged an abolition mindset toward her financial situation—a mentality that doesn't involve police and prison.

"Righteousness doesn't get you very far," she said. "Can we actually lean into abolition in this moment? Can we lean into it as a practice?"

"What can I do to protect the next black woman who gets targeted?" she asked. "I really want to create a blueprint for protecting black women leaders specifically."

The audience clapped but not quite strongly enough. Her interviewer was a friend and fellow activist, Nikkita Oliver.

"Yes, clap for that," Nikkita said, then added, with a firm tone in her voice: "Like we said, we're here to protect black women."

Nikkita said it's racist that Black Lives Matter is getting so much scrutiny. "Hello ACLU, you all got money, but nobody's asking for their 990s."

For Patrisse, the tax code around charities was upsetting and almost a sort of violence.

"I actually did not know what 990s were before all of this happened," Patrisse says. "So part of the opportunity here is to educate our folks. Something's being weaponized against us that many people don't know and honestly don't care about. The accountant handled that. I don't know what that is. It is such a trip now to hear the term *990s*. It's like ugh, it's like triggering."

Nikkita completely agreed.

"I think that's why so many folks avoid the nonprofit industrial complex. When we think about our movements for black liberation, in order to serve community quote-unquote 'legally,' too often do we get pushed or forced into a system that is actually meant to attack us and limit the capacity and reach of our work. I think we have to start questioning those institutions."

The audience cheered. Patrisse picked up on the energy of it. People wanted to hear about her trauma.

"There has been so much questioning for me. I'm like, 'Wow this doesn't seem safe for us, this 990 structure, this nonprofit structure, this is like deeply unsafe, like, this is being literally weaponized against us, against the people we work with. I can't tell you how many people are like, 'Am I next? Are they going to do this to me?'"

After Patrisse stepped down, BLM was a zombie bank account without a known leader. Two leaders stepped up to guide the organization—Minyon Moore and Marc Elias, old hands from Clinton-world. Within months, they quietly stepped away as well. Neither gave any interviews about the time, and didn't respond to my questions. Then the organization's board was composed of three little-known figures: Cicley Gay, D'Zhane Parker, and Shalomyah Bowers.

BLM issued a "transparency" report in 2022. My favorite is

this line item: "$3 million of 'stimi' COVID relief funding given directly to Black people." There's no explanation beyond that. Some people, somewhere, during COVID, were given $3 million.

"Like a giant ghost ship full of treasure drifting in the night with no captain, no discernible crew, and no clear direction," said CharityWatch executive director Laurie Styron. Indiana's attorney general called BLM a "scam" organization, and California's Department of Justice sent a warning letter to the organization for failing to submit the proper nonprofit forms for 2020. BLM was banned from soliciting more donations in the places it stands to raise the most: California, for one, and then New York's attorney general Letitia James banned them from soliciting there as well. (Now BLM is back in action, accepting more donations.)

On the corner where George Floyd was actually killed, the intersection that set off these years of rage, there was for a while another small autonomous zone, another police-free utopia, in a town with another progressive mayor.

The streets had been closed off with more makeshift barricades. Burned-out trash bins, metal roadblocks, and plywood preventing anyone from driving or walking in without an assessment. The autonomous zone extended about a block out in all directions from the corner where Floyd had been killed. Guards installed prefab guard houses in the middle of the road, and they walked out to inquire when anyone approached. Police were not allowed in, and neighbors said police cars refused to go even within a few blocks' radius of the new land. Ambulances of course were not allowed in. Most media were also not allowed in, unless they were known to be sympathetic. Volunteer guards periodically emerged and told camera crews to get the hell out. I walked in on a cold spring day, ten months after the killing.

A young man stepped out of the guard house and stopped me. He was white and wearing a well-kept handlebar mustache and his shirt unbuttoned to the stomach, showing a hairy, muscular chest (it was March and a little chilly).

He said he was "holding space for the community to ideate." He crossed his arms, kept a wide stance, and wanted to know where I was from and what I was doing. I said I was a reporter with *The New York Times*, which was true at the time. Our paper had just that morning called the square *sacred*. He let me in, with a nod and an alright.

Handlebars didn't want to share much about himself, but another guard was more forthcoming. He was also white, wearing a beanie, with thick-gauge earrings. He was a special education teacher at a local Minneapolis public school and was doing this because, he said, he wanted to defend the community. Many schools were shut down still from the pandemic, so he had a lot of free time. He felt called to fight, and the way he could help was making sure Fox News was kept out.

The area had a surprising number of visitors. They wanted to see the corner where the police officer killed George Floyd. They wanted to pay their respects. Visitors were often parents and their children, from all around the country.

A black family with three young kids said they drove out from

Chicago to pay their respects. We stood together at the pile of flowers where George Floyd had been killed. The father, Terrance, told me he was teaching his children about history, that "there's always a better way."

People roamed about, soliciting donations to the cause of Black Liberation via Cash App.

Kids came up to me selling Black Lives Matter rubber bracelets for five dollars. Others sold flower bundles to lay on the corner. Next to graffiti reading FUCK THE POLICE were foot-long QR codes—point your smartphone camera here and a website would pop up, urging visitors to give to that variety of newly launched black American causes with chic websites.

The tent marked MEDIC was, inside, just piled up with firewood and garbage bags.

The gardens with tomatoes, peppers, beans, and herbs had received glowing international coverage of their own—"A Garden Is The Frontline In The Fight Against Racial Inequality and Disease," said NPR—but it was cold and they were now just dried-up sticks. People were sitting around a fire pit by the old gas station.

Part II

ATONEMENT

Speaking Order

I once had an on-camera job at a trendy media company in Brooklyn. And anytime I had an idea in a meeting, a slightly younger man would repeat what I'd said and people would remember the idea as his. A mediocre idea of mine suddenly became gold when a young man spoke it. It was an odd thing, a microaggression if you will, and it drove me wild. I complained, as I love to do, but nothing was changing. So I came up with a dark solution: Before a meeting, I'd give my ideas to my handsome male producer, and he would pitch them. It worked beautifully. It drove me crazy. But it worked, and there I was getting on camera.

But it's not fair. It's not right. I'm told this even happens to other women. It should not be thus. It might not be the biggest problem, but it is a problem and fixable and maybe fun to fix. And so there are efforts to fix this and other conversational hegemonies.

One way to fix it is a clever system to figure out who speaks first at events in progressive spaces (political gatherings, academic conferences), and it is called the Progressive Stack.

The stack is simple: Those most oppressed speak first. Then, the moderately oppressed. Last, the least oppressed. Oppression is obviously connected to race, so black people should be at the front of the line, then Latino people in order of descending skin tone. But there are also disabilities to consider (visible and invisible), gender identity (trans before cis), and then sexual identity (gays before straights). But it gets messy: Would a white gay guy go ahead of a straight Asian man? Is a trans teenager more oppressed than someone in a wheelchair? I imagine them having to fight so we can figure it out. Whoever loses wins. But how it actually works is that the Progressive Stack moderator will be called to help figure out who should be in front, and who behind.

When people line up to ask questions at some Democratic Socialists of America conferences, a moderator walks through the line moving some to the front and some to the back, to follow the Progressive Stack.

The idea is that people whose ancestors have had enough time in the sun of power should wait a beat and let others speak. The stack ought to inform all facets of someone's life. In class and in social conversations and at work, a good progressive follows the stack, a sort of modern chivalry. Everyone is generally good about supporting the stack and knows that it is good.

From the DSA's Guidelines for Respectful Discussion: "If someone who is of an oppressed group or identity, or of a group or identity that is unrepresented in the conversation raises their hand, they go to the top of the list."

Speaking order "is one way to address and practice the reversal of systemic inequities introduced and held by white supremacy and patriarchy," says the Othering & Belonging Institute at the University of California, Berkeley, in their *Bridging & Breaking: Dialogues of Belonging* workbook:

> Speaking Order is often difficult to explain. . . . To introduce Speaking Order, you might say something like: "We are going to practice shifting the power dynamics today. We will use Speaking Order as a way to reckon with our shared history of imperialism and a white ruling class. . . . We acknowledge that there can be discomfort around this ask regardless of your positionality or 'situatedness,' but invite this practice as a model for authentic reconciliation and as a path to increase mutual Belonging.

Sometimes very good progressives don't want to be at the back of the line. It doesn't quite seem fair. Sometimes adjustments are made. Sometimes sacrifices are made.

To change your spot in the stack is not a casual venture. I am not talking here about a progressive who accidentally cooked tacos then claimed to be a little Mexican to avoid a riot among their friends.

To truly change your spot in the stack requires changing your whole life. It requires denying your parents and cutting off your siblings. But sometimes adjustments have to be made. Especially if someone is a very good progressive doing very good work for the cause. Then being at the bottom of the stack can feel just not fair at all. If your cause is righteous enough, climbing the stack can feel very, very right. Which is how a lot of white women—maybe with curly brown hair or vaguely, slightly at a certain angle, Latino features, maybe with an uncanny ability to do a Black American accent or pull off traditional Native American necklaces—rose to the very, very top. Andrea Smith had a long, illustrious academic career as a Native American professor specializing in Native American women's issues, working as a professor at the University of Michigan and later University of California, Riverside. She was a prolific activist—she cofounded INCITE! Women of Color Against Violence, Chicago's chapter of Women of All Red Nations, and the Boarding School Healing Project. It did unfortunately turn out that she had most likely lied about her native heritage, and she agreed to "retire" from her teaching position at UC Riverside.

Or there's Kay LeClaire, also known as nibiiwakamigkwe. A leader in the local Indigenous movement, Kay had claimed Métis, Oneida Nation, Anishinaabe, Haudenosaunee, Cuban, and Jewish heritage. Kay, who goes by the pronouns they/them, was a co-owner of giige, a "Queer and Native American-owned tattoo shop and artist collective in Madison, WI." They were a Community Leader in Residence at UW–Madison's School of Human Ecology and was part of the Missing and Murdered Indigenous Women Task Force. They have had copious speaking engagements, and they even led a name-change mob, forcing a local music venue Winnebago to change its name for Indigenous sensitivity (it was named after its street). They sold crafts and clothes, all while saying she was Native American. They also claim to be Two-Spirit, a sort of nonbinary identification long practiced in Native cultures.

Unfortunately, they are in fact German, Swedish, and French Canadian. An anonymous blogger identified the fraud. On a related note, the self-reported "Native American" population in the US between the years 2010 and 2020 nearly doubled.

Jessica Krug, a tenured associate professor of history at George Washington University, pretended to be Afro-Latina, even faking an accent.

Many of these people cut out their families to continue their deception. They created entirely new lives. They had friendships and fell in love as their new identity.

Why would people work so hard to take on an ethnicity that's not theirs?

There's power at the top of the stack. There's prestige. If you want to study a culture now, you have to be part of that culture (i.e., it's *problematic* for a white professor to write about non-European history). If you want to write a novel about an ethnicity or group that's not your exact ethnicity and group, you're in trouble. And, yes, there's money. Activists get prestige, and they get funding.

An "Emancipation Conversation" I was invited to was sponsored by Shell. Businesses reinforced the stack and quickly absorbed social justice language. A billboard outside a bedding company in Brooklyn read: "Black trans rest is resistance." The multinational bank HSBC made an ad featuring a genderqueer person applying mascara: "Gender's just too fluid for borders. HSBC: Opening up a world of opportunity." Your money and your gender know no borders.

A real announcement from a venture capital firm: "Capital Factory welcomes you to our LatinX in Tech Summit presented by Accenture!"

Any jobs or sponsorships had to be part of achieving justice. When the Duke and Duchess of Sussex joined Ethic, a fintech asset startup, they told the *Times* that they "hoped that their involvement would help democratize investing." Buying a hat from Alexandria Ocasio-Cortez is about solidarity: "Each article of Shop AOC merch signifies solidarity with the movement." It was a moment for the culture to take advantage of too: When HBO Max relaunched *Gossip Girl*, it was still about elite New Yorkers, but now, the showrunner said: "These kids wrestle with their privilege in a way that I think the original didn't." He cited Occupy Wall Street and Black Lives Matter: "In light of [Black Lives Matter], in light of Occupy Wall Street, things have shifted."

The Central Intelligence Agency got in on it too, releasing a new set of recruiting videos with agents describing their various identities: "I am a woman of color." "I am a cisgender millennial." "I have been diagnosed with generalized anxiety disorder." "I am intersectional."

Princeton's class of 2025 is 68 percent non-white. Now that could be genuine diversity, or it could be that many people stand to gain a lot by taking a 23andMe and identifying with that 2 percent.

Some minority groups became too assimilated, and then it was unclear if they were a minority anymore, metaphorically speaking. The executive director of the AAPI Equity and co-founder of Stop AAPI Hate spoke about how Asians need to check their "anti-blackness" and "white adjacency."

"Toni Morrison spoke about this years ago in a piece she wrote on immigration. Which is that, sadly, immigrants come to the United States often and understand right away the racial hierarchy that we have in our nation. And so they know that if they want upward mobility, if they want economic security, they need to align themselves with whites, essentially," said Manjusha P. Kulkarni, who also lectures at UCLA. "And so you see a lot of that sort of white adjacency in our community or efforts to strive toward white adjacency."

No one wants to be white-adjacent. If the stack is the new way, no one wants to be at the bottom. A stack may have put my pitches ahead of my mediocre colleague's. But not by much. I'd need to play up my womanhood. What exactly counts as a disability, again? I need to at least get into the middle.

The Most Important White
Woman in the World

What are the characteristics of white people? A middle-aged white woman named Tema Okun with flowing long hair created the definitional list. In that list she put *perfectionism, a sense of urgency, worship of the written word, a right to comfort, individualism, one right way,* and *objectivity.* Those were white values, Tema said. These were how white people upheld their supremacy.

This observation from Tema was considered by many very smart people to be deeply anti-racist, which meant it was good for black and brown people. The idea was that white people in good standing needed to always be aware when they were exhibiting or enforcing these white values, and also that black people don't share them.

In this worldview, if black people do somehow exhibit urgency or perfectionism, it means there has been internalized whiteness. And that is a type of death for that black person.

Tema Okun's list briefly became one of the most important documents in America—another kind of constitution for a certain set of civic leaders. The characteristics are used as lesson guides by some of the largest nonprofits in the country, by huge school districts, by universities, by the Smithsonian National Museum of African American History and Culture, and by the Democratic Party. The list has reshaped schools and policies across the country, changed how newspapers operate and how therapists do their work. The list has flourished, permeating our lexicon. It has sprung into a thousand anti-racist training programs. Videos of peppy white people describing the traits of their own white supremacy abound. The Gates Foundation funds work that explicitly builds on Tema's list to bring it into education—specifically math instruction.

Tema Okun helped make justice work personal. If racial injustice is actually because of culturally taught and internalized differences, then the fix is also internal and emotional. White people have *a sense of urgency*; that's white, Tema said. To create a more equal society, white people need to work on deprioritizing their urgency. Justice work is not about gathering a bunch of ladies to do letter-writing campaigns for Iranian women or some such. It's about having them pay to become less interested in urgency.

Most Americans have never heard the name Tema Okun. They have never read the list of traits. Not many people have, really. But we are all beginning to live in the list. By 2020, Tema's arguments were the mainstream mode of justice work.

When public health officials in Oregon needed to delay a meeting, they did not simply say they were running late or that the materials weren't sorted yet. A high-ranking official wrote, citing Tema's work: "We recognize that *urgency* is a white supremacy value that can get in the way of more intentional and thoughtful work, and we want to attend to this dynamic. Therefore, we will reach out at a later date to reschedule."

The Smithsonian Institution—along with the National Museum of African American History and Culture—made and disseminated a big poster based on Tema's list, riffing a bit. *Rugged individualism* is part of *White Culture in the United States*, the poster reads. *Timeliness* is white culture. *Objective, rational, linear thinking* is white culture. *Self-reliance* is white culture. Being *action-oriented* and *future-oriented* are both white culture. The *nuclear family* is white culture.

Tema's list was especially a hit in math classrooms.

"A lot of practices that are commonplace in a lot of math classrooms—not all, but in a lot of math classrooms—are aligned with a lot of these white supremacy characteristics," Rachel Ruffalo, who is the senior director of Strategic Advocacy at the Education Trust-West, tells me when we talk. Education leaders worked to overhaul California's entire K–12 math instruction around the characteristics. California's proposed new math curriculum framework, released for public comment in 2021, recommends teachers refer to: "A Pathway to Equitable Math Instruction." Here's what the Pathway says:

> Our systems expect math teachers to prepare students for what is more easily measurable, reinforcing both *quantity over quality* and *sense of urgency*. Also, many teachers prefer to teach procedural fluency so students engage with more complex problem solving because they believe that they have to do the basic, or computation, skills before they can apply the mathematics. But that idea also reinforces *objectivity* by requiring a singular path for learning, which is oftentimes not necessary. This is related to *sequential thinking*, without interrogating the need for that particular sequence of learning. In addition, many teachers are more comfortable teaching skills-based work, and if they do that more often, they are reinforcing their own *right to comfort*.

(In 2023, California's new math curriculum, slightly watered down, did pass. It became law of the land for the whole state.)

Anyway, those are white values, and expecting those values to be shared was racism, Tema said, and God, did that feel right to a lot of white people. Anti-racism was about unpacking those white values. Doing so is hard emotional work for white people, deep internal work. Work that acknowledges that everyone in the room is always rushing so much, is so demanding of ourselves, so exacting, so white. Work that is best done over some sauv blanc.

"What happened was I came home very frustrated after a meeting, a dynamic meeting where a lot of the characteristics were showing up," said Tema Okun. "And I sat down and the words just poured through me onto the page. I didn't wrestle to find the words. The words found me."

The list arrived in the world in 2001 as a paper with a simple name: *White Supremacy Culture*. The original paper had two authors. Kenneth Jones, a black anti-racist educator, and Tema Okun. Kenneth died in 2004. Since then Tema Okun has been written as the list's sole author. She explains now that this is how it always should have been.

"I—Tema Okun—wrote the original article on White Supremacy Culture in 1999," she posted on her website. As for Kenneth: "When I originally published it, I listed him as coauthor because so much of the wisdom in the piece was a result of our collaborative work together. When he realized I had named him as a coauthor, he demanded that I take his name off the piece, claiming he didn't want credit for something he didn't actually write."

The '90s anti-racist scene was bustling with curious new nonprofits and radical collectives. The tree-lined blocks of Berkeley, California, were a hotbed of it all. There were Challenging White Supremacy Workshops and the People's Institute for Survival and Beyond, both of which Tema cites as the foundation for her work.

Many meetings took place in lovely Berkeley living rooms—I imagine old Craftsman homes full of books, with richly painted walls—where activists held salons and struggled with each other. They taught that white people were not a neutral state, with everything else being *ethnic*. Whiteness was just as much a racial identity as blackness. These ideas were radical and are still compelling and true. For a white-skinned person to assume white is the default means being unaware of your own strangeness. It's like assuming everyone's Christian, that Christian is default and that Christmas isn't religious but sort of neutral. To live like that in a diverse society, one with lots of Jews or Muslims, makes you at least a bit of a jerk. And so it is with race. Assuming you're neutral limits you, and makes you clumsy out in the world.

Sharon Martinas, the cofounder of the Challenging White Supremacy Workshop, wrote a history of that program for posterity. Who was there? Again, white women. "Workshop participants were mostly white, college-educated, working and middle class grassroots social justice activists between the ages of 20 and 30. Approximately 90% of each workshop class of 30 were women."

The Workshop's trainings were focused on getting white people aware of global liberation movements and teaching them how to help. The gist was: *We're lucky here in Berkeley, let's now make things better for people in other places, in whatever ways we can.* The women worked hard at it. They envisioned a Third Reconstruction that would mean radical reparations to the formerly enslaved. On international issues, these women were being trained in how to support leftist movements in Cuba, Puerto Rico, and Mexico. Some would then travel to those places, bringing attention, know-how, and material aid with them.

It was exhausting and difficult work, and in 2005, the program closed in chaos. It was just too hard. It was too much work.

Sharon wrote: "Once, an all white small group criticized the workshop for not allowing them enough time for processing. Their spokesperson was a young woman with blond, curly hair. I looked at her in confusion after she offered her criticism. 'Processing'? I repeated. 'Excuse me, but this is a workshop, not a hair salon.'"

Reflecting on what went wrong, Sharon explained that the movement members wanted more focus on themselves. "'Back in the Day,' white activists and activists of color believed that the revolution was around the corner so our pace of activity was frantic. Many of us felt we weren't serious revolutionaries if we worried about 'taking care of ourselves.' Today, many white activists prioritize taking care of themselves as revolutionary work."

"At the time, I felt like my life as an anti-racist solidarity organizer was finished and that I was a failure," Sharon wrote. "This self-definition as a 'failed revolutionary' was not a particularly functional place from which to ask the obvious question, 'So what do I do now?'"

Sharon felt like a failure.

Tema, who was in the mix with Sharon and her comrades, was rising. Tema had a different plan in mind.

⬚

Born in 1952, the daughter of a well-known progressive professor at the University of North Carolina at Chapel Hill, Tema rebelled against what she saw as an overly intellectual family life. She went to Oberlin and majored in physical education. "I knew it would freak my father out if I was a P.E. major, because it was anti-intellectual. So those three things kind of converged, and I became a P.E. major," she said of the choice. She started a graduate degree in sports medicine at Chapel Hill but failed the training exam and never finished her degree. (Later, she went on to complete a PhD at the University of North Carolina at Greensboro, with a thesis titled "The Emperor Has No Clothes: Teaching About Race and Racism to People Who Don't Want to Know.")

After a breakup, she moved to Seattle, worked as an aquatic and fitness director for a local YMCA, and got into the clogging scene, joining a group called the Duwamps Cloggers. She started working in the anti-racism world, and she liked it, eventually partnering with anti-racist educator Kenneth Jones.

When they worked together, Tema was often in charge of details like plane reservations. Kenneth didn't care much about details. She would get upset and feel resentment, creating what she described as a relationship of *"beloved-ness and tension."*

But Tema always stayed a little different from the others in that alphabet soup. They were all too focused on formal non-profit structures and minutiae, she thought. They were focused on just what was right in front of them.

Tema was having a spiritual experience. One night, after a frustrating day seeing a lot of bad white behavior, Tema sat down and something *"came through her."*

"I operated mostly as a vessel and the words came through me rather than from me," she wrote in 2021, in a self-published retrospective about the list. "The original article was my one and only experience of producing something that came through me."

The document was so simple. The list was so clear. It did not ask those white women to learn about Puerto Rican political figures. It did not tell them to phone bank and mail letters to their congressmen or get on a plane. It told them to release their perfectionism. It told them that urgency itself was white supremacy.

Under Tema, the anti-racism movement could shift from a political movement grounded in facts to an emotional and spiritual one. The battle did not need to be about structural realities and governments. It could be about ourselves. Objectivity—facts— it's all racist. Whiteness is a virus that kills.

"The purpose of white supremacy and racism is to disconnect us from each other," Tema said one day during a talk with a reverend. "To disconnect each of us from spirit, source, creativity or whatever you name the energy that connects all of us. White supremacy and racism are designed to disconnect us from the earth, the water, the wind, the sky, the sun."

The goal of Tema's work is not necessarily to raise up black and brown people but to take down the white supremacist system. It is not to add more diverse faces at the boardroom table but to dismantle the table.

"The underlying assumption is that this white world is the default world, the normal world that we should all aspire to," is how she put it to a crowd at a conference once. "This white world is in deep trouble. What we need is an entirely new table or perhaps no table at all."

This is what made Tema different from the rest of those Bay Area anti-racists. It's why it was so powerful.

"An assumption of racial equity work in the past was that racial justice was to the benefit of people of color, and we're going to lift people of color into the white world, and that's the goal," Tema says, in a keynote address to a data science conference called JupyterCon. "And what I see changing, which is really, really critical, is that more and more white people understanding that that's not the goal. This is not about simply including people into the white world. It's about questioning the world." She has a lean face and long gray hair. She speaks slowly, carefully. Sometimes she holds her hands together as if in prayer.

Whiteness, to Tema, is like the serpent. She calls it a "constant invitation" that has to be turned down.

She often talks about anti-racism in openly religious terms. And the new anti-racism has been embraced by a liberal Christian world that articulates whiteness as a sort of satanic possession—an original sin. The anti-racist movement grew, and the scenes were familiar Christian scenes. In June 2020, white police and activists in Cary, North Carolina, washed the feet of black protestors and asked for forgiveness.

Some anti-racist training programs are semireligious organizations, sometimes explicitly. One diversity training program with four locations around the country was called Crossroads Ministry. They've since rebranded as Crossroads Antiracism Organizing and Training.

Tema makes appearances to religious bodies. She appeared with the Reverend Tami Forte Logan, a preacher with the African

Methodist Episcopal Zion Church. The event is put on by Grace Covenant Presbyterian Church in Asheville, North Carolina. The event began with the audience being asked to breathe deeply together.

In the recording, Tema comes on in a purple blouse, a gray sweater over it. There's children's artwork behind her. The room is dark but she is lit, which is how she styles most of her appearances.

The Reverend Tami, who is black and younger than Tema, says when white people are exhibiting the traits of whiteness, they seem crazed.

"From the outside looking in, I've observed that often unfortunately it almost looks like a possession, like something just takes over white people," the reverend says.

Also there is Pastor Marcia, who is white and with Grace Church. She agrees.

"What is it that makes whiteness so seductive?" Pastor Marcia says. "It internalizes itself in white bodies but also black, indigenous, and brown bodies. It gets into our cells. It changes the way our bodies work. What is it about this that is so seductive that we literally eat it and drink it and let it seep into our bones?"

Whiteness seeps inside her. She's drawn to it, and she hates it.

When someone gives in to that temptation for whiteness, they die, Tema says. Anyone can drink of whiteness. Anyone can die of it.

"People from different ethnic communities that end up giving up their ethnicity in order to join whiteness, it is death. It is completely death and the actual suicide, addiction, depression, all those rates are much higher in the white community, and I think there's a direct connection," Tema said. "We have this sense that we are involved with something that is so wrong and bad."

Freedom from the traits of whiteness is the goal. Freedom from the urgency, freedom from the written word, freedom from perfectionism. These are white values, and we can be better and happier without them.

"This isn't about helping others," Tema says. "It's about how my life, my happiness, my belonging depends on helping to enact racial justice in our world."

Pastor Marcia agrees.

"Tema, I want to say hallelujah," Pastor Marcia says. "I see white people being set free from their own bondage."

I emailed Tema, asking if she'd have time to connect and talk about the document and its impact. I quickly got a phone call from an anxious man who is not Tema. He is a public radio reporter and a friend of Tema's just wanting to know what I'm up to, exactly. I said, I'm just interested in Tema's work and influence and would love to learn more. He asked why. I said, because it seems like she made an important document. He told me it's "conspiratorial to think Tema is very influential." He said she's "just a woman" living her life and "she's shy." After the call I got an email from Tema:

Thank you for reaching out to me. I do not want to talk about
my work; I just prefer to do my work. Thank you.
Tema Okun
she/her
from my iPhone

Then quickly another:

And I apologize if I sounded short. I am distracted by the
aforesaid work. I wish you happiness in yours.
Tema Okun
she/her
from my iPhone

The public radio reporter had mentioned that Tema was busy
getting ready for a twenty-year commemoration event to celebrate the document and its impact later that week, so I signed
up. The contact email was whitepeople4blacklives@gmail.com.

Tema had said she knew that the White Supremacy Characteristics needed to be updated after two decades in the world.
First, resistance against the list itself needed to be added to
the list.

"It badly, badly needs to be updated," Tema told supporters.
"For example, I and my colleagues have come to see other central elements of White Supremacy Culture that need to be named:
Fear. The idea of Being Qualified. And Defensiveness needs to
be broadened to include Denial."

She would unleash the update to the list at this event. A thousand people showed up for the big reveal.

A racial equity strategist started the meeting with a poem about separating colors: "We dare white light to pass through a prism and separate light," the reader said. "We dare the rainbow of colors to weep."

And then there was Tema, speaking slowly and quietly in another darkened room. She had some news. Unfortunately, Tema announced, she wasn't finished. The new characteristics would be late.

Urgency is white supremacy, she reminded the audience.

Everyone understood.

What I Heard You
Say Was Racist

It is time to correct her, and we know how to do it by now. We have spent days learning how to break white solidarity. We know we have to find the edge of our discomfort.

We, each in our own homes but gathered for days of Zooms, have to find the shake inside ourselves. Passing on this chance to reflect means sitting quietly in our white-bodied privilege, and bodies of culture people don't have the option to sit out being harmed. The correction shouldn't be given apologetically or packaged with niceties. Whiteness manifests in controlled, polite speech, and we had practiced passionate speech.

Stacy knows it's coming.

"Who would like to give Stacy direct feedback?" says our facilitator, Carlin. "I see Claire. I see Emma. Great. OK, Stacy, what's happening in your body right now?"

Stacy is an older white woman with long straight gray hair who says she loves swimming. Right now, she is scared.

"My heart's beating," she says. "My throat is a little clogged." She says she's about to cry and that she's focusing on breathing deeply.

"Great," our coach says. "You have the privilege to open consciously." Once open, Stacy can hear feedback now. She can be a more responsible white person.

Carlin gives the go-ahead for a woman named Chloe to give feedback. Chloe is talking to herself, getting herself amped. We are a group of about thirty people, mostly women, all white. Now we are in a major learning moment, because Stacy said she was ashamed of being white and that she hoped in her next life she wouldn't be white anymore.

"'Grounding, rooting, removing Bubble Wrap,'" Chloe says rhythmically, before looking directly ahead: "Stacy, what I heard you say about wanting to come back as a dark-skinned person in your next life was racist because as white people we don't have the luxury of trying on aspects of people of color."

"Notice how challenging that was, Chloe," our facilitator says. "That's what getting your reps in looks like."

A woman named Dori comes next.

"I'm sweating. My heart is beating. I feel shaky," Dori says.

She says Stacy's words felt like they were exoticizing people of color. She says it felt like Stacy saw people of color as better or more desirable. She says Stacy's statement was "an othering."

Our facilitator pushes her for more. Sum it up in one sentence, she says. "When you said that you wish you would come back in your next life as a dark-skinned person, I experienced that as racist because. . . ."

Dori swallows deeply.

"That was racist because it exoticized black people."

It was *romanticizing*. It was *extractive*. It was *erasing*. It was *like she was shopping*. Our facilitator chimed in on the assessments pushing for more from everyone, and more came. For a few minutes, Stacy is a representative of white-body supremacy. (Later, it will be me.) We all need to be shown the harm of our ways. If we don't do it, we will continue to cause harm to bodies of culture.

Stacy sits very still. Eventually we finish.

Our facilitator asks us to raise our hands if we had wanted to protect Stacy during that. A lot of us raise our hands. It's a perfect example, she says, of white women's tears in action. "White women's tears, how they can hijack a space and people immediately want to step in, like it's a biological thing, a reflexive impulse."

And how is Stacy? our facilitator asks.

Stacy says she is just very grateful. She is grateful that she was asked to stand on her own, since white comfort degrades us both.

"Somebody isn't trying to take care of me," Stacy says, her voice thin. "Thank you."

This is the second of four days of a course held in May 2021, called, "The Toxic Trends of Whiteness," hosted by Education for Racial Equity and facilitated by Carlin Quinn, featuring a talk from Robin DiAngelo. After this class, I will go on to another course, "Foundations of Somatic Abolitionism." That one will be more about what my white flesh itself means and how to physically manifest anti-racism—"embodied anti-racism." Those sessions will be co-led by Resmaa Menakem, a therapist, trauma expert, and former radio show host.

Robin DiAngelo is the most prominent anti-racist educator working in America. Her 2018 book *White Fragility: Why It's So Hard for White People to Talk about Racism* was on the *New York Times* bestseller list for years. During the heat of the Black Lives Matter protests, DiAngelo's influence boomed, sending her book back again to the top of bestseller lists, reaching number one. She was brought in to advise Democratic members of the House of Representatives. Coca-Cola, Disney, and Lockheed Martin sent their employees through DiAngelo-inspired diversity trainings.

In the DiAngelo doctrine, there are not individual racists doing singular bad acts. All white people are racist, because racism is structural. We are socialized into it from birth. To fix one's inherent racism requires constant work and it requires white people to talk about their whiteness. To do so they must identify as white.

She's right that white is seen in America as the default, blank, neutral, not racial at all. Anything else is viewed as *racial*. To me,

DiAngelo is right in many ways. There was obviously structural racism in this country, laws for example about where Black and Jewish people could buy property, laws that have impacted who is rich and who is poor for generations. The laws may be gone, but there's obviously still racism in America today. The idea here is that one way of challenging that racism is white people sitting among themselves to think about all this and work through it.

"Part of the reason why I'm doing this work is so that bodies of culture don't have to," Carlin tells us. "Working within white community can be incredibly hard, draining, and harmful. And there has been an ask from my colleagues that white people work together."

Exposure to standard levels of racism could harm a black teacher. That's why, for now, the anti-racist teachers are often white.

The course begins with easy questions (names, what we do, what we love). And an icebreaker question: What are you struggling with or grappling with related to your whiteness? We need to answer in a way that puts skin in the game—"as close to the bone as possible, as naked, as emotionally revealing," our facilitator says. It should be uncomfortable to share.

One woman loves gardening; her spring garden is popping up right now. Another woman loves the salt water and says she's calling in from her family's beach cabin. People say they feel exhausted constantly trying to fight their white supremacy, that it's like a current pulling them under.

A woman named Mia introduces herself. She is a white woman with a biracial child and says she is scared that her whiteness could harm her child.

Claudia says it's frustrating that white women were fighting patriarchy for so long, and now, just as that seems done, she feels like she's lost to her whiteness.

"It's like, here I am ready to speak my truth and sort of being told to step aside." She wants to know how to do that without feeling resentment.

Claire lives in the Los Angeles area and loves her cats. "What I struggle with is how to understand all the atrocities of being a white body," she says, "being a privileged white supremacy person." Knowing that her very existence perpetuates whiteness makes her feel shame and fear, and she worries she's a drag on society. "The darkest place I go is thinking it would be better if I weren't here. It would at least be one less person perpetuating these things."

Beverly says she feels uncomfortable now around other white people. "When I'm around white folks, I feel weak."

Evelyn, who loves gardening and her daughter, is scared of being mocked.

"I'm almost afraid now to do anything because I'm afraid of being a middle-aged white woman and being called a Karen." Anything she does, she's just a white woman who's a problem.

Evelyn saw a book the other day "that was basically about Karens." She was surprisingly triggered by it. "I think it's really for me about finding a place and how to deal with the hate and the fact that I'm white," she said. She knows that's a huge problem.

She knows her race has created "this settler colonizer society." So that's why she's here. That's what she's grappling with.

Emma, from San Francisco, goes next. She is already crying. "I'm here because I'm a racist. I'm here because my body has a trauma response to my own whiteness and other people's whiteness."

Nora, who works in nonprofits, is struggling to overcome her own skepticism. "Some of my natural reactions are kind of instinctively skeptical."

Our facilitator picks up on that: How does that skepticism show up?

Nora continues: "Wanting to say, 'Prove it. Are we sure that racism is the explanation for everything?'" She gets nervous.

Her anxiety and tension here is good, our facilitator says. It's OK. It's good to get to the edge of honesty and vulnerability. It's OK to get to the point where you almost want to throw up.

"It's really an important gauge, an edginess of honesty and vulnerability—like where it kind of makes you want to throw up," our facilitator says.

Claire loves nature and works in student services. She feels "perpetual shame" that she isn't doing enough. She lists her perfectionism and fear of conflict. But she's woken up recently to her whiteness. The trouble is now she feels paralyzed. But she knows her silence also makes her complicit.

Another woman is tearing up. She is a diversity, equity, and inclusion manager at a consulting firm. She struggles with how to help people of color but also how not to take up space as a white person. It's a pickle, having to center whiteness and de-center whiteness at the same time.

The conundrums, the riddles, are part of the work, our facilitator says.

"We want to understand with compassion and also develop a culture of accountability." We are trying to stop doing something that causes a lot of harm to a lot of people.

The next day we hear from Robin DiAngelo herself in a lecture format. Our facilitator introduces her as "transformative for white-body people across the world."

Robin is wearing a mock turtleneck and black rectangular glasses. She's quite pretty. She starts by telling us that she will use the term *people of color*, but also that some people of color find the term upsetting. She will therefore vary the terms she uses, rotating through imperfect language. Sometimes "people of color," other times "racialized," to indicate that race has been done to someone. Sometimes she will use the word *BIPOC* (black, Indigenous, people of color), but she will then make a conscious grammatical mistake.

"If I say BIPOC, I find that's a kind of harsh acronym. I usually add 'people' at the end to humanize it a bit, even though grammatically that's not correct," Robin says.

Next, she wants to remind us that she is white. She emphasizes strongly on the *wh—*, giving the word a lushness and intensity. *White.*

"I'm very clear today that I am *White*, that I have a *Whhite* worldview. I have a white frame of reference. I move through the world with a white experience. Probably one of the deeper challenges of trying to educate white people is our lack of humility. If you are white and you have not devoted years, years—not that you read some books last summer—to sustained study, struggle, and work and practice and mistake-making and relationship-building, your opinions while you have them are necessarily uninformed and superficial.

"Challenge number two is the precious ideology of individualism, the idea that every one of us is unique and special."

She prepares us for what comes next: "I will be generalizing about white people."

She throws up an image of middle-aged white women.

"This is the classic board of a nonprofit. I want you to imagine the neighborhoods they likely grew up in, the schools they likely attended. If they are married, what did their albums look like?"

She throws up a picture of high school students in a local paper with the headline "Outstanding Freshmen Joined Innovative Teacher Education Program." The teenagers are white.

"This education program was not and could not have been innovative. Our educational system is probably one of the most efficient, effective mechanisms for the reproduction of racial inequality. I think we all know that, or we would not care so deeply about what schools our children go to."

Lingering on the picture of the teenage innovators, Robin asks us: "Do you feel the weight of that whiteness?"

She stares ahead. She holds her fingers together into a triangle. Another image. It's a white man.

"I don't know who that is," she says. "I just Googled 'white guy,' but most white people live segregated lives."

As we work, Robin tells us that when someone calls a white person out as racist, the white person will typically deny it. It will go something like this, Robin says:

"Denying, arguing, withdrawing, crying, 'I don't understand,' seeking forgiveness, 'I feel so bad, I feel so bad. Tell me you still love me.'"

She pauses.

"Emotions are political. We need to build our stamina to endure some shame, some guilt," she says. These should be temporary feelings as we understand racism as a system.

Our facilitator says that intentions are the province of the privileged. But consequences are the province of the subjugated.

Robin lists the ways that one can strive to be anti-racist. Someone who has integrated an anti-racist perspective should be able to say: "I hold awareness of my whiteness in all settings, and it guides how I engage. I raise issues about racism over and over, both in public and in private. It's integrated into what I think about and notice and see and care about, and so if you hang out with me, that's what we talk about. You want to go watch a movie with me? You're going to get my analysis of how racism played in that movie. I have personal relationships and know the private lives of a range of people of color, including black people. And there are also people of color in my life who I specifically ask to coach me, and I pay them for their time.

"Now, at the 101 level, I think it's really healthy to just defer to the guidance of whoever, whichever person of color is in your life as a white person."

There is a book she suggests we read called *Why I'm No Longer Talking to White People about Race.*

The book's written by Reni Eddo-Lodge, or as Robin says, "a Black Brit." For a moment she looks scared. "I hope that's not an offensive term."

Our facilitator, who has been on mute, chimes in: "I think it's OK."

"It sounds harsh. The Brit part sounded harsh."

Robin's time with us comes to an end.

Our facilitator asks if we have questions. Very few people do. White bodies have nothing to say about a profound presentation. Silence and self-consciousness are part of the problem. People need to push through. We need to notice excuses. "People's lives are on the line. This is life or death for bodies of culture." So we need to notice what edge we're willing to get to. Only by getting to the edge of our comfort can we engage in anti-racism.

"The semantics of whiteness are unconsciously driven by white superiority and this entitlement to exist and a right to thrive that's inherent to the white body," our facilitator says. "This right to thrive. This physical entitlement to space. There is a deep impulse to go for the things we want."

"Whiteness is like an octopus," she says. "It has its tentacles in everything. It's far reaching. It's slippery. It's smart. And when it doesn't like something, it clouds the space."

We have, by this point, learned several tools for our embodiment practice. One is humming. And so now we all hum together.

We need to work on handling criticism. Our facilitator calls it getting activated.

A woman named Vanessa raises her hand. "Right now I'm shaking."

That's good, we have learned. It's OK to shake.

Emma has a question. How can linear thinking and perfectionism be white? She wonders if that might be more of a personality trait since her husband and son don't seem to be perfectionists, but they're white. Then she wonders why she is wondering this, whether the question itself is white supremacy.

Linear thinking is part of the colonized mindset, our facilitator answers. Linear thinking is privileged and prioritized over nonlinear thinking. Indigenous ways of thinking and speaking tend to be more cyclical and more storytelling.

A man named Alex says he felt uncomfortable with Robin talking about how freeing it was to identify as a racist. Here he'd just been talking to all his friends about *not* being racist. Now he's going to have to go in front of people "and say that I might have been wrong here." He is noticing he is "feeling resistance to saying 'I'm racist.'"

Our facilitator understands. It's OK and normal. So he just needs to try again. Say, "I am a racist." He should say it and believe it.

The man says: "I am racist."

What does he feel?

He says he feels like his body or his heart is trying to accept it, trying not to fight it.

Say it again.

"I am racist," he says.

What does he observe? Any emotions or images, any temperature changes, any tightness?

Alex is tearing up.

"Do you feel sadness or grief?"

"Sadness and grief feel true," he says.

"That's beautiful," our facilitator says. It's OK to sit with that. As a practice for the next two days, we need to take a moment, different moments throughout the day, and say to ourselves, "I am racist." And let it land in our bodies. See how it feels. "I am racist."

Someone confesses that they tattled on a coworker who was habitually late. She feels awful. It's just her feeling "that sense of urgency," which is so hard to escape.

I'm late one day coming back from our lunch break. I get in a little trouble. It doesn't matter if I say I'm sorry, our facilitator tells me. I did it. And expecting to be able to waltz back in having missed content, well, "there's whiteness in that." Can I accept that?

I ask if there's any way to catch up on those minutes of missed material.

That would be extra work for our facilitator so no. Asking that is an example of how whiteness functions.

I feel horrible.

In a small group session, a woman tells me how hard it is realizing how much suffering she must be causing her non-white husband.

She is "constantly perpetuating this toxic whiteness at him." And he is the person she loves more than anyone in the world. Yet here she is, hurting him. She feels helpless.

One woman says she's scared to do the "feedback" training when we give corrections for white supremacy.

Our assignment is to give feedback that we don't want to give. "In a way that makes you shake," our facilitator says as a day of classes wraps up.

It's very important that this work start in white communities. This work can be hard in white relationships. It can certainly hurt your feelings. But you're not going to be harmed by it. Processing your whiteness with a person of color can cause harm.

"Remember, my body is socialized to white comfort," our facilitator says. "So if we're comfortable, there's a good chance there's white supremacy at play."

Fixing this is not a to-do list. It's not a workshop. It's a way of being, our facilitator says. It is "a rehumanization" process "to reclaim aspects of our humanity that our ancestors relinquished."

We learned that we need to identify as white bodies. Everyone else is a body of culture. This is because white bodies don't know a lot about themselves. "Bodies of culture know their history. Black bodies know."

You have to have skin in the game, which means you have something to lose. Something that's on the line.

Stacy, after her correction, is having a breakthrough. She is rocking and humming to herself. "I'm seeing them finally," she says. "Like, wow, are there moments when this white body chooses to see a body of culture when it isn't dangerous for them?"

Ilene realized that she is "a walking, talking node of white supremacy."

Ellen is upset. "I just was not conscious of the impact."

Jana's aha moment was realizing how vast whiteness is. "So vast and so, so big."

The course featuring Robin DiAngelo as guest speaker ends. The next course features Resmaa Menakem. Our facilitator remains the same. She says that Resmaa always tells her something really important about bodies of culture versus white bodies.

"He says, 'We're good.'" Bodies of culture have their traditions. They have community. They have access to wholeness. White bodies do not.

Resmaa Menakem is a somatic abolitionist. The author of *My Grandmother's Hands: Racialized Trauma and the Pathway to Mending Our Hearts and Bodies,* he grew his profile off appearances on Oprah's and Dr. Phil's shows. He advocates for something called *somatic abolitionism,* which he describes on his website:

> Nearly all of our bodies—bodies of all culture—are infected by the virus of white-body supremacy. This virus was created by human beings in a laboratory—the Virginia Assem-

bly, in 1691—then let loose upon our continent. It quickly infected people of all culture and pigmentation, backgrounds, and economic circumstances. Today, the WBS virus remains with us—in the air we breathe, the water we drink, the foods we eat, the institutions that govern us, and the social contracts under which we live. Most of all, though, it lives in our bodies. Somatic Abolitionism heals our bodies of the WBS virus—and then inoculates our bodies against new WBS infections.

Before we can abolish our whiteness, we need to feel our white skin. We need to activate it. Our facilitator is there to help get things started. We tap gently and lightly on our skin. On our chests, our hips, our feet, our backs, everywhere we can reach.

We are "activating containment." We are activating our vessel. We are activating our flesh.

Then we do a foot massage. Some people do it for a few seconds and then stop, waiting for the next instruction. That's not right.

We're told to work with each individual toe. We need to stick with it. We need to give good, strong squeezes. And then gently slap slap slap the bottom of our feet.

We just hear the slap slap slap of hands on the bottom of feet. If we think we're too cool to engage, our facilitator will check in with us.

Thirty more seconds.

We break out into small groups to talk about privilege other than our whiteness. I am paired with two lovely white women named Sarah to confess our privilege. "I have thin privilege," says one of the Sarahs.

⬚

As I'm writing this, there are dozens of panels and workshops every month working on these issues.

There is a dinner series for white women to talk about their racism that for a while was very popular. The hosts—Saira Rao and Regina Jackson—encourage women to abandon any notion that they are not racist. The program is called Race2Dinner, and a dinner during the height cost the host somewhere around $5,000; a ticket went for $625. They publicized with a simple message:

> Dear white women: You cause immeasurable pain and damage to Black, Indigenous and brown women. We are here to sit down with you to candidly discuss how *exactly* you cause this pain and damage. The dinners are a starting point. A place to start thinking through how you actively uphold white supremacy every minute of every day. What you do after you leave the dinner is up to you.

One could also attend the workshop called "Unpacking Sexism and White Privilege in Pursuit of Racial Justice," hosted by the authors of *What's Up with White Women* (the authors are two white women). Or you could go to "White Women Taking On Our Own White Supremacy," hosted by Finding Freedom (a for-profit run by two white women). The National Association of Social Workers' New York City chapter advertised a workshop called "Building White Women's Capacity to Do Anti-Racism Work" (hosted by the founder of U Power Change, who is a white woman).

Almost all of the workshops are run by and aimed at white women. There are almost none geared toward white men. White women specifically seem very interested in these courses. And white women seem particularly thorny for the anti-racist movement. The hated archetype is the Karen. There's no real equivalent for men (maybe the heavily armed prepper male comes close, but it's not quite the same, in that a Karen is someone you'll run into in a coffee shop, and a Karen is disgusted with herself). There's a way in which this type of self-flagellation is uniquely female. Where another generation of white women worked to hate their bodies very, very much for gaining a little cellulite around the edges, my generation effectively hates our ourselves for any vestige of "whiteness" (and I don't mean skin color necessarily, as this can also be your internalized whiteness; while the Karen crosses races, the Karen is always female). There is endless demand for women to apologize a little bit for something and women love doing it. Women will pay for the opportunity. We'll thank you after.

We find our "spine of dignity."

We start to sway. This is embodied anti-racism. Our facilitators tell us we are like snakes. Our spines curve and twist. We should begin to rock. When you push yourself too far to the edge, just rock in place. We do three communal hums to settle the nervous system. Resisting the rocking, feeling embarrassed, is part of white-body supremacy. Being guarded, ungrounded, frozen in our bodies, and cut off from our hearts is normal and typical in white community.

Resmaa comes on with a low, rhythmic voice. He shows an image with arrows out of Africa indicating the slave trade.

"My ancestors were and are tied to creation itself," he says.

He tells us to keep looking at the image.

"Something happened. Things continue to happen to those people. These black bodies were not immigrants. They were enslaved."

Over and over he says it: Something happened. His voice is mesmerizing. Something happened here. Things continue to happen. I start to hear the sound of it. For a second I'm overwhelmed by the rush of violence it all was. I'm overwhelmed by how cruel people are. And he keeps going: Something happened. It's awful. I start to cry.

"It's going to take nine generations before white bodies even know what the hell race is because they have been advantaged by it for so long," Resmaa says. "With rough calculations, that's about how much time we've been in this racist culture."

He is speaking slowly to us.

"All white bodies cause racialized stress and wounding to bodies of culture. Everybody say it. 'All white bodies cause racialized stress and wounding to bodies of culture.'"

I say it over and over.

"Notice the rage, the sadness. All white bodies can learn to move and speak in ways that cause less stress and wounding in bodies of culture."

One woman is crying. She has a southern accent. There is a piano behind her. "I feel like I'm experiencing the pain that I have caused black and brown bodies."

Resmaa continues slowly, repetitively. *Pause, pause, he tells the woman. Pause, get some reps in. Deepen your discernment. That energy has four or five hundred years of charge to it. It can blow through brown bodies. Do you understand what I mean?* He tells us to move when we're anxious, rock like we're holding a baby.

"Just slow it down. That's what I call a primordial wiggle."

"For most of our history, the white body has had full and un-fettered access to every orifice, every idea, every understanding, every part of the black body. White bodies are conditioned to expect my deference."

He's been working lately with adoptees, he says, rocking to heal the feeling of crossing water. He spoke recently to a national organization on gynecology: "Nobody is talking about the impact of historical trauma on the womb."

We do more humming, and then some "warning and ward-ing." We bare our teeth. We look in each other's eyes. We growl a little. We bare our teeth again.

He warns us not to try to teach this to others. People have been stealing his curriculum, but it can be dangerous.

He says we need to find two other bodies of the same race to do this with and commit to doing this with them for the next three years and then for the rest of our lives. These groups cannot be mixed race.

"Do not do mixed triads," Resmaa says. "Do not have bodies of culture in a group of white bodies. White bodies with white bodies and bodies of culture with bodies of culture."

"All white bodies cause racialized stress and wounding to bodies of culture."

Monica has a question about community-building. She is scared because she has a mixed-race group of friends, and she wants to be sure she's not harming the black members of her group.

Resmaa says it's impossible to do this work with them.

"There's no way you're going to be able to keep black women safe. If you're talking about race, if race is part of the discussion, those black women are going to get injured in the process," Resmaa says.

"That's my worry," she says.

"This is why I say don't do mixed groups," Resmaa says.

She's sad. "These are, you know, it's like an anti-racism study group."

"Don't do that," Resmaa says. "I don't want white folks gazing at that process."

Resmaa leaves us with a warning.

"Some of you may lose spouses. Some of you may lose friends. You're going to have to pay the price. If you're not open to that, then what you're doing is performing. If you tell me you're an ally, I say: 'Who are your people? Who are the people holding you accountable? Who are the people you're naming children with?'

"Begin to temper and condition your body to be able to withhold and withstand the charge that comes."

He invites us all to the upcoming two-day workshop.

There is no escape. If you feel uncomfortable or claustrophobic, that's good. I felt claustrophobic within myself for days after.

At one point in the courses, a man named Jack raises his hand. He says he was realizing that his white-body-ness was far deeper rooted than he knew.

"Maybe I do need to occasionally be scolded," he says, "for assuming I have a right to a particular position." People who don't have white bodies probably feel scolded a lot. Maybe it's OK to feel on the other side of that, he says. Maybe it's part of healing.

But now he's been thinking: "How deep does this go even?" Where does his whiteness end and his personality begin? "Or are they entangled from the root?"

They are, Carlin says.

"That makes me a little anxious," Jack says.

Whose Tents? Our Tents!

Never mind the Mexicans. Never mind them outside their condos, complaining.

This park had been blessed. It had been chosen as a campsite. Hundreds of people from around the country came here to this corner of Los Angeles to live and show their freedom and the work was to help them. They had chosen this lake and this park in this gentrifying Mexican American neighborhood now sprinkled with whitewashed multimillion-dollar Spanish houses repainted and filled with fiddle-leaf fig trees. People like me who buy those fresh white houses with fiddle-leaf figs in the staging know we owe a pound of flesh back. I would be lounging in that

Latino neighborhood in that Latino park and know I owed something back. And here it was. The homeless had come two hundred strong. They had moved into the park, and protecting them was an opportunity.

The Democratic Socialists of America could help—they could organize this group and grow it. This was an opportunity. Points could be made here in this park. This community could become an example of how homelessness is not a problem to be fixed with something simple like housing. Actually, the homeless should not be housed at all. At least not yet. Homelessness is a tool of the revolution.

"They call us Invisible People, like we don't exist," one member of the camp says in one of the many promotionals the group puts out. "But if something happened, if they needed some help, we'd be the first ones to help them because we're representing God."

"Imagine a world where there was no 'bottom,'" the camp wrote in a fundraising letter. "One where your neighbor was your neighbor because they're your neighbor not because of tax brackets or real estate. A world where good is done for the sake of good not gain. In the past few months, we, the unhoused community at Echo Park Lake, have been creating the groundwork for this world."

In 2021, it was getting harder to make noise marching. The events were losing steam. But if BLM was fading, there were other communities to galvanize. If the goal of the amorphous new social justice movement was to show the rot in modern culture, to show the hypocrisy and insanity, to demand revolution and the end of capitalism and to make suffering impossible to ignore, there was no better group of people to use than those who were living on the streets. The rallies could move into tent cities. And activists could move into tents too.

Echo Park is a chic Los Angeles neighborhood with a lot of microbreweries and skyrocketing home prices. The neighborhood is about half Latino and a bit more than a quarter white, and that's been changing fast. The namesake park of the neighborhood has been a sweet, somewhat run-down spot with swan paddleboat rentals for lazy weekends. That park went through a $45 million makeover a few years ago, and it became a jewel. It's the neighborhood's backdrop, where quinceañeras and brides have their photo shoots.

And in 2019, as real estate prices spiked, so did the population of a small tent community. Soon, what had been a few tents and tarps ballooned into a village. And when the pandemic started, efforts to dispel the little town fell away.

They called themselves the Echo Park Tent Community. "The biggest pandemic in years actually turned out to be a blessing for us," they said in a statement. "Without the constant LAPD and city harassment uprooting our lives we've been able to grow."

The homeless camp became a community. People came down from the hills and the hip houses to service the tents. Every day, attractive young helpers showed up with food, and solar panels to charge the encampment phones. It became a hub for Los Angeles's Democratic Socialists of America chapter. It was helpful that the park is in a convenient location, a hip neighborhood where many of the DSA types had moved to recently anyway.

The tent community created their own rules. The police didn't intervene in many disputes, locals told me, but the community appointed their own security team, young men who wandered with skateboards.

The tents filled the grassy hills. They filled the lawns. The residents set up barbecues and outdoor living rooms with leather sofas and fluffy La-Z-Boys. They set up makeshift water bottle showers and dug holes to use as bathrooms.

The tents were built right up to the nice paved walkway. Walking through the village, it was like walking on a narrow European street, though instead of apartment buildings, there were family-sized tents crowded along the sides.

As word spread about the new park turning into a tent village, new homeless arrived. Volunteers from local Los Angeles non-profits would greet them and give them new tents, sleeping bags, hot food, and clothes. Newcomers to the camp would be given jobs within the community, often paid for by donations. So the homeless (or unhoused, as we should say now) would have jobs cooking and cleaning or be in charge of trash pickup. There was a young performance artist named Paige, who called herself a "housed neighbor." She is "an embodied gardener and plant practitioner" and describes her work as something that "bridges poetics and praxis, mysticism and theory, healing rituals and environmental science." With all those qualifications, she helped run the community garden.

Some residents settled in and began expanding their fief-doms, using a couple of tents, one to sleep in, one as a living room. They had pets and decorations, flags and mannequins.

Some of the residents set up solar panels on top of their tents. There were tarps making shaded lounge areas and stacks of nice bikes. An outer layer manifested—a permanent wall of camper vans.

Sometimes the police came to try to clear away barbecues or chastise someone whose encampment had grown just a little too big. When they did so the activists would descend with smart-phones. It's unclear if it deterred the cops or not. But the police would eventually leave, dragging a few items behind them sort of randomly, as if to say *Oh, this bit went too far.* Eventually, the police decided to more or less ignore the place.

Anyone living in a city in the American West is now seeing homelessness as part of their life. None of this is news. When I moved into my house, there was someone living in a tent a block away. It's a big family-sized tent that takes up the whole side-walk. A month later, I noticed there were two tents. Six months in, there were four tents and a full living room spread out on the sidewalk. Sometimes there's no tent. Sometimes there's half a dozen and a fire pit.

When I walk by our small encampment, I'll stop and see what's going on. They usually have stacks of food, left by one of the city agencies or soup kitchens that bring hot food to clusters like this. More often than not, a few residents are on the side-walk, and they're perfectly polite and perfectly stoned.

These are my neighbors, and I want to help them. I've always voted yes on every homeless housing supplement I come across in every ballot.

My housed neighbors want to help too. Blue city voters have so far proven willing to spend more on the homeless. Los Angeles had spent and was spending a lot of money getting shelters together. Los Angeles approved a bond measure for $1.2 billion in 2016 to build housing for the homeless. They were told it would mean 10,000 units of housing for the homeless. Five years later, the city had only completed a fraction of them. One project cost $837,000 to house each resident. The comptroller described the costs of construction as "staggering." That money went where all California's massive budgets go: to overpaid city contractors, convoluted union deals, and incompetent spending. And despite all the money, the unsheltered homelessness in the city increased 14 percent from 2022 to 2023. A homeless woman with a knife disrupted an LA mayoral campaign event focused on homelessness.

With housing that hard and expensive to build, and with the pandemic making it a bad idea to shove people tightly into shelters, cities like Los Angeles and San Francisco started a parallel program that was easier—no need to build anything. The city would just pay for homeless people to live in nice hotels or let them take over parking lots or parks. City officials would wander through Echo Park offering residents rooms in those hotels.

But the rooms came with rules. There were curfews. Residents could not do drugs in the rooms. And the rooms were, of course, indoors. People high on meth and fentanyl prefer being outdoors, with no rules, with their friends. I asked one man why he likes being in an encampment instead of being housed. He looked at me like I was an idiot: "It's more fun," he said.

Then came word from the city. In March 2021, the Echo Park encampment had to go. Residents would be offered housing and then the park would be fenced up to prevent people from moving in.

Activists—who had organized under the name Echo Park Rise Up—made beautiful fundraising videos showing children playing next to the homeless. They dismantled a city-funded water fountain and announced now it was a community shower.

During the days everything did seem fairly stable. A family posed for a wedding photo shoot, angling the bride to miss the tents.

The most media-savvy member of the encampment was a handsome, thin young man named Ayman. He has long hair, a charming smile, and a bouncy gait. He would frequently feature in videos promoting the Echo Park encampment. It was a media production house of a homeless camp, and the tents had signage. One read: WE REFUSE TO BE SWEPT INTO DARK CORNERS. Ayman's tent had a Bernie Sanders flag.

"It seems in this world there are two types of people," Ahmed says wistfully in one promo video. "The type of people where love and empathy comes simple but power structures and hierarchies come hard. Then the other type of person is where love and empathy comes hard for them but power structures and hierarchy comes easy."

Ayman talks in the video about the community as an effort to get back to the Garden of Eden and the childhood playground. There's a small wooden sign in the encampment with just the word REDEMPTION written across it. A sign in the garden reads: "We are all of nature." Another: "Radical gardening: Community, kin, symbiosis, intentionality, care, presence."

As evening fell in the park, it got a little rougher. Residents fought; women shouted over territorial disputes. Fights over drugs were frequent.

Deviations from the script could be seen. One resident, a former model who moved to the park, posted a video of himself screaming into the camera as his leg bleeds from a gunshot wound.

Sometimes the housed neighbors would get upset about the situation. They missed the lawns, they said. They didn't feel safe, they said. There had been deaths in the park. There had been sexual assaults.

Andrea Martinez Gonzalez grew up in Echo Park and worked in a courthouse in downtown LA, mediating civil harassment. She's in her seventies now, a progressive voter. "I'm not afraid of socialism," she said. But the park worried her. There'd always been a few people sleeping in it but something different was going on.

"I saw them building a kitchen and I said, uh-oh these people are here to stay. Many of these people are ne'er-do-wells, a lot of drugs, a lot of mental issues. I also noticed some young hipsters who wanted to live off the land like Thoreau. Even though Echo Park has now become quite gentrified, there still are a lot of families here and this is their park where they'd go picnic with their children and it became a place where you didn't want to expose your children to that," she said of the encampment.

She said she knew kids who couldn't use the park anymore. "We have a family of five children in a one-bedroom apartment and they're a great family. They stopped going to the park and that was their only respite from getting out of that one-bedroom apartment," she said. "They stopped because they saw lewd and disgusting things going on."

When she was a kid, she said, the park always had gang members. "There were gangs, but they respected women and children. We never had an issue. There wasn't this public display of penises flying in the wind."

What finally put her over the edge was when she saw one of the tent-dwellers crush a baby duck in the middle of the day: "I said, this is it."

Andrea wrote what she describes as a "diatribe" on Nextdoor, a neighborhood-based social network. She wrote it in Spanish because she figured that would make it harder for the park leaders to call her a white supremacist.

One night, an eighteen-year-old girl with a big smile came to volunteer at the camp. An honors student, marathon runner, and violinist with curly brown hair, Brianna Moore had grown up in the small town of Oceanside, north of San Diego. She'd had mental health troubles and had gone briefly to a hospital, according to her family, but also had run the Los Angeles Marathon twice and was set to start college that fall. She came to LA hoping to get involved with the left-wing action—the George Floyd protests mostly, but also the Echo Park effort at building a better world.

After the police first started trying to move the encampment, a group of local leftists had been living at the camp with the addicts, and she appeared to be joining the crew.

Soon after, she was discovered dead in a tent. I reached out to my local city councilman, Mitch O'Farrell, about her, and I got through to his spokesperson, Dan Halden. Dan told me that what was really strange was that it appeared Brianna's dead body had been moved from tent to tent over a few days. It looked like Echo Park residents had cleaned up. No one in the park would talk about what happened.

They hadn't even called in about her death, Halden told me. Her body was found by someone walking past the tent and noticing her there. Her feet had been sticking out of a large maroon and white camping tent, set up on the manicured lawn right by the pond. The police report just says: "an anonymous passerby was walking on a walkway and checked inside the decedent's tent for unknown reasons."

Someone took a video of the police wrapping her body in a white sheet in the middle of the day. The wind is shifting the tarp around. She's alone in there. By then, she had been dead for up to three days. The autopsy report noted "early decomposition with ant activity." There was cocaine and fentanyl in her blood.

After that, noticing the glare of bad local press, the park activists planted a community garden right by the water where her tent had been.

"She was inspired by the movement. She wanted her voice to be heard. She started off with a good crowd that wanted to help people, and over time, she just met the wrong people," her sister Jill told the local TV reporters.

The *Los Angeles Times* called it "a commune-like society," but a lot of locals didn't feel like members. A small Change.org petition sprang up run by a new anti-encampment group, Friends of Echo Park Lake. The signatories wrote notes. Sandy writes: "I want to be able to take my sons for an evening walk without fearing for our safety." Rocio: "Signing because I feel unsafe at and around that area." Marya: "I want to be able to take my family to Echo Park, it's not safe anymore."

Jose Miguel Portela Iglesias remembers one night when there was a protest. A Christian singer was staging a worship service and performance in Echo Park on New Year's Eve. The DSA members started to clash with his fans. And in the middle of the ruckus, there was someone dead, floating in the lake.

"Floating! Can you imagine. With people pedaling by on the boats," Jose said to me. He lives right off the park.

"It's not socialism. A lot of these people that came to the park they were white rich kids from other neighborhoods. They came here and they claim being socialists and being pro-homeless and they came with vegan food and, like, expensive white rich kid food. It was a party. Every night."

High-end restaurants from Silver Lake and Echo Park would

donate food. Many mornings, Jose says, there were boxes of French pastries.

Apparently the pastries were only for the deserving. The truly desperate homeless camped separately from the more political hipster inhabitants. The donations didn't make it to the truly desperate, Jose said. "The food went only to the middle where these kids were playing being activists."

There were activities. Once a week was a drum circle. Jose's girlfriend, Nicole, listed other activities. "There was an organic garden, they would DJ off of iPads, ride skateboards."

The activists who planned these events were well-meaning, she said. "A lot of young, really passionate, intelligent people had a lot of time on their hands and they got caught up in the fever," Medine continued. "They wanted a cause so badly. If these homeless people had been housed, they wouldn't feel important anymore, and they wouldn't have the limelight."

When city workers would come through to throw out trash, the activists formed a human chain to block them.

She said she personally saw the volunteers paying homeless people to stay in the park. She called the homeless outreach program Street Watch "the gestapo."

The Echo Park homeless community organizers did not like the locals complaining. They tracked down the people who signed thatChange.org petition. They showed up at the home of one signature gatherer. And they called the workplace of another. She ended her involvement in the effort after that. She couldn't lose her job.

"You've heard about Jed, right?" my local council member's office asked when I called asking about the park (I've become a very annoying new resident). "You have to know about Jed."

Jed Parriott became the Echo Park homeless camp's self-appointed leader. He's in his late thirties, white, with sort of puppy-dog eyes, often wearing T-shirts and hoodies. He pops up all over the city. "We're here to say no to this luxury housing going up on Skid Row," he says to the camera one day in 2017, standing on the sidewalk holding a sign that reads: "Say 'no' to skyscrapers on Skid Row." His hair is tousled, though by the time the Echo Park city rose, he was balding.

Parriott was, in the parlance of the community, "a housed neighbor." He comes from a well-off LA family; his father is James Parriott, who did some producing and writing on *Grey's Anatomy*, *Sons of Anarchy*, and *Ugly Betty*.

Parriott the younger showed up many days at the Echo Park camp. He was busy. He was managing PR and operations for a lot of homeless efforts. He'd pull up to Echo Park in a BMW X5, a detail I first saw reported in *Los Angeles* magazine, which broke many of the details of what was going on at the park. I could hardly believe it.

He was the organizer squaring off at public meetings, leading the fray in a contentious neighborhood informational session, holding the mic up for a homeless friend.

When groups of trendy young people came from around the city to face off with the cops, there was a good chance Jed Parriott was helping organize. Some in the city government suspected Parriott and his crew were paying the homeless to stay in the park instead of going into shelter. I don't know if I believe them. But he did discourage people from going into shelters. He called the shelters "carceral," saying they're prisonlike because they have strict rules around curfews and drug use. There's truth to it: The project to get folks into those hotels was called Project Roomkey, but no one got a key to their room. When they wanted to get back into those rooms, they were escorted from the lobby.

Parriott is a take-no-prisoners kind of debater.

"We need to be really telling these property owners, 'Sorry, you're going to have to tough this out,'" Parriott told KABC-TV News. "I'm sorry that you don't like that you have to see this, that you have to see poverty."

At one community meeting, he faced off against a representative of a neighborhood group that wanted the encampment cleared, according to several locals who were at the meeting. The resident introduced herself and said she lived in a senior home and used to walk in the park but now doesn't feel safe. About fifty people were in the old church for the meeting. Parriott talked about how this is just something everyone would need to accept.

"He said he knew people didn't like seeing poor people, but that was the way it was going to be now," one local told me.

During a vigil for those who died on the street, Jed was clutching a black woman to his side and holding a microphone for her. She was on crutches. He was in a beanie and green jacket.

Over time, he began to talk as though he too were homeless. It would be easy to forget that he showed up in the BMW X5.

"That night, we thought—I say, we, the residents," he said to *Street Roots*. "We got word that they finally put up a paper notice at the park saying the park was going to be closed at the very moment riot police surrounded it."

"You can't just kick us out," Parriott said to the *Los Angeles Times*. "Until you find and address the actual problems and actual solutions, I'm sorry, but we're gonna be here."

In a Los Angeles Board of Supervisors meeting about how Los Angeles should handle encampments, Parriott was there at the microphone.

"We are actually in the streets, a lot of us here talking," Parriott said. "We know what we're talking about. And we know that what you're talking about is exactly the opposite that needs to be done. So what's driving this? Is Donald Trump driving this? Because to support this motion is to stand with Donald Trump."

He singled out a black member of the Board of Supervisors. This supervisor had apparently been a little too frustrated with the homeless situation.

I want to ask you, Mark Ridley-Thomas, do you want to stand with Donald Trump? You know your recent tweets kind of indicate maybe you are standing with Donald Trump. So tell us where do you stand? Do you stand with Trump or do you stand with us? Do you stand with fascism or do you stand with real solutions?

Ridley-Thomas sounded bemused. He responded in a calm, deep voice.

"OK," he said, and the audience laughed a little. "If you confuse me with Donald Trump that's going a long way in the wrong direction."

In another meeting, Parriott took the stage to chastise Supervisor Janice Hahn and demand private land be taken.

"It was disappointing to hear you, Janice Hahn, mischaracterize Services Not Sweeps," he said. "You're talking about 'we want rent control'? You're too late on that. And so we're going to have to take much more radical measures unless we want to see people living in encampments for decades. We're going to have to start expropriating and using eminent domain to take property."

It seemed like a plan that would be less expensive than new construction—simply seizing existing property. (The lawsuits might add a significant price tag.)

"If you don't like that you have to see people living in tents, you should be mad at the people who forced them to have no option but to live in a tent—that's the capitalists, the real estate folks with all the money and power and the politicians and police that serve and protect them. Racial capitalism has created this," Parriott said in *Street Roots*. "Folks should be angry at the system."

It was Parriott who urged protestors to gather nightly as the date of Echo Park's clearing approached. One night they held a candlelit vigil for the homeless, hundreds of young activists walking around the lake and its tent city clockwise. They were quiet and somber. They were honoring the encampment.

A writer from *Vice* was there in support; so was an editor from the *Los Angeles Review of Books*. An eco-musicologist was there. Some reality TV contestants were there. A young actor was writing in support: "What the city has done to Echo Park Lake is just heartbreaking." A *New York Times* columnist responded on Twitter: "I agree. And it makes no sense."

That night, protestors faced off against police. The whole East Side of Los Angeles was loud with the sound of police helicopters. Some protestors came in black bloc, a nod to the more hard-core scene in the Pacific Northwest. But most were there in normal street clothes.

"Fucking piggies. Cover your nose! Cover your nose, you fucking losers!" a young woman yelled at officers. Another young woman shouted at a line of officers: "Christopher Dorner was a fucking hero." (Dorner was the former Los Angeles Police Department officer who in February 2013 shot five police officers, two fatally.)

The police did a clever trick. They told protestors: *Alright, fine, we won't clear folks out tonight. Everyone gets one more day.* As protestors went back to their homes, the police wrapped the park in a fence. No one could come in. All they could do was leave.

Protestors who came back in the morning were horrified to discover they were locked out. They started putting signs up on the fence.

"Every border implies the violence of its maintenance," one sign read.

When the police finally did clean up the encampment, they found 35 tons of waste, with a literal 180 pounds of crap. They also picked up 30 pounds of needles, 3 firearms, and untold knives and machetes.

The fence stayed up longer than the park residents stayed in shelters. A lot of park residents went into housing for a short period of time; many or most of them left that housing soon enough and scattered.

And Jed Parriott disappeared entirely.

He stopped tweeting. He didn't respond to any of my requests to talk. But someone like Parriott can come in and out. He can have his years in Echo Park and then get back into the BMW X5 and off he goes.

When I landed in Los Angeles one night, I stopped in the women's room by baggage claim. In the stall next to me was a woman who was unconscious, splayed out.

I knew she was probably just drunk or zonked on drugs. She was fine. I knew that. But I couldn't stop looking at her arms there. She could have grabbed my ankles if she wanted to, but I knew she wouldn't. I could call 911 to get her help but she'd get in trouble of some kind.

So I left her there.

A few paces out I stopped. What if she was dying? I had a family member who died on the bathroom floor. What if she was dying and I just left her?

So I let the nearest airport agent know. She looked at me with a smile. "Yeah, the homeless," she said, and went back to her phone. So did I.

A little while later, I got an email from my local neighborhood group that included a rundown of various safety and security incidents in the area. It was a pretty typical month. One item stood out to me:

> Officer responded to a call of a person floating facedown in a pool. It appeared the person drowned. It was a local homeless person who has been seen many times in the area. No foul play.

We Mean, Literally, Abolish the Police

All the smart people are buying guns. That's what I told myself waiting in line for one. The shop owner said he'd get someone to help me, and a sweet and clearly gay woman was sent my way. We nodded in the way two lesbians will, and I said, "I guess I'm here for a gun."

I'm not totally unfamiliar with guns. I was in charge of making squawking noises with the duck call when Dad went hunting, but I've never wanted to bring one into my house. I'm uncoordinated and weak, and I always figured if there was a gun or even spray involved in a tussle, it wouldn't take much time before it was used on me.

But things kept happening. A woman with her newborn was followed home and robbed in the middle of the day, just a few blocks from me. A friend's mom was murdered at her home during a botched burglary in a much nicer neighborhood than mine. Then another home invasion near me. Then another. It made me pause. It made me a little scared. There are so many windows in our house, and at night I started to think about each of them a lot. Did the baby's room need bars? When I forgot the keys in our car's cup holder one night like a fool, the Honda was gone from our driveway by morning.

A friend told me that he called the police once and they said they'd be to his house in forty minutes—*Forty minutes! Can you believe it?*—but I thought this was hyperbolic. Then one night our alarm went off (we had gone to see a movie, it was a false alarm, nothing taken). By the time we got home, it had been going for an hour. We stood in the dark backyard and realized that if something happened, no one was coming.

When we bought our house in central Los Angeles, I talked to someone who knew the previous owner. I was gushing over how I couldn't believe anyone would move out of this place, and she looked at me really seriously. *You do know what happened to Lauren, right?* Lauren is who lived here before. I didn't know what happened to Lauren, no. *Just woman to woman,* the lady tells me that the reason Lauren moved her family out in a rush and sold the house was because someone had broken in and was living in the house while the family was on the road. *And it was really strange—he stole a lot of photos of the children and stole their passports, and I thought maybe he was stealing their identities.* (Of course, everyone in the neighborhood ended up having a slightly different story.)

A few weeks later I got pregnant. Almost as soon as I peed on a stick, I got in the car and found myself holding an AR-15, getting a sense of the heft.

Is a shotgun better because of the wide spray? That seems good in a panic. Or a pistol because it's nimble? Easier to carry as we jump out the window. Buying a gun is a little like signing a prenup. You suddenly have to consider all nice things only as their most evil iterations. Which window am I most likely going to see a rapist jump through and what placement of the gun safe makes sense for that? Could that overgrown rosemary hide a killer as we walk into the house?

By the end of my first trimester, I'd learned how middle-class and upper-middle-class homeowners stay safe in Los Angeles. It's expensive.

First, an ADT alarm system. Alarming the house with ADT, the largest security company in the country and a pretty standard pick, cost us a few thousand dollars—ADT's hardwired cameras were another few thousand—plus there's an $80 monthly fee. You stick a bunch of those signs in the front lawn. But then of course there's the issue that no one shows up when the alarm goes off.

In our neighborhood, a rich swath in the middle of the city, next to the ADT lawn signs there are the Black Lives Matter and In This House We Believes. And then, more often than not, there's a fourth sign: Armed Response.

So we pay another $250 a month into the shared community

patrol—for that armed response—and former police officers will show up when our alarm goes off. When you first sign up, they come over to visit. Our visit is an older black retired cop in a private security uniform. He's sweet and reminds me never to call 911. Just call him.

Private security guards are armed off-duty cops and military veterans, and they're most certainly not wearing body cameras. As police fail to provide timely services, these private guard companies have boomed around the country. There are twice as many private security guards in America today as there were twenty years ago.

So for a few thousand up front and $330 a month, I can live as though there are police. I can feel quite safe. No one is really bothered by this. Another armed patrol service sends me an email asking if I need the new, more expensive concierge security service, which they are launching due to "overwhelming demand."

It's not exactly hard to hate the cops. After all, they have—or at least are meant to have—a monopoly on violence. The job often draws an aggressive personality type. Now add to that: with video, we have a better idea of how often they're screwing up. And they screw up a bunch. We can see it now.

It's a video of a man crawling down a hotel hallway, drunk, desperately trying to follow directions but also—here was his mistake—trying to pull up his pants. It's a video of that man being executed. It's cops pulling up to a playground and killing a little boy within two seconds. When those cops are held to account, even with the videos showing what looks so obvious (an execution), more often than not they can claim it was an honest mistake and get off easy. There might have been a gun in his pants, they can say. The toy gun looked real, they can say.

With the help of bystander video and body cams, defunding the police—Better yet, abolish them! Abolition now!—went from a fringe wild idea to the very center of American progressive politics and it went there fast. Within what felt like weeks in the hot summer of 2020, it seemed like every liberal organization, every media company, every nonprofit became an "abolish the police" lobbying group. The fight for clean water or abortion access or equal pay became a fight also for police abolition, and these could not be untwined. Other causes would become similar all-encompassing obsessions, but for a couple years the line was: environmentalism is police abolition; pro-choice begins with police abolition, etc. Police abolition was exactly what it sounds like but it was also about a revolution.

"Defunding the Police: What It Means and Why Planned Parenthood Supports It," wrote the women's health and abortion rights group, who, you would think, had enough battles on its plate given that just a year or so later *Roe v. Wade* would be overturned.

The American Civil Liberties Union joined in too: "Divest from police and reinvest in the Black and Brown communities they unjustly target."

The nonprofit Sunrise Movement, established to galvanize young people to fight climate change, was now mostly a police abolition movement: "Defunding the police is just one step towards abolition. We're hosting a 4 day crash course to deepen our understanding of abolition and learn how we can take steps toward defunding police." *Atmos*, a magazine dedicated to climate change, laid down the stakes: "There's No Green New Deal Without Police Abolition."

A community organizer for the climate-change awareness nonprofit 350.org wrote: "Even if you don't understand *how* at the moment, you gotta know that abolition is the only way forward . . . we first have to recognize that we have to abolish. We'll figure out the complete 'how' together, leaning on the teachings and writings that already exist, by trying stuff out locally, and sharing lessons."

The Democratic Socialists of America came out strong for abolishing the police. It was common to see signs like those held one day by members of DSA Chicago announcing the agenda: "DISARM. DEFUND. ABOLISH." More moderate think tanks like New America joined in 2021: "Why Are We Afraid of Defunding the Police?"

Legacy media was there to buoy the movement.

The New York Times gave space to the opinions: "Yes, We Mean Literally Abolish the Police," wrote the anti-prison activist Mariame Kaba in June 2020. And another: "No More Money for the Police."

The Atlantic chimed in with "Incremental Change Is a Moral Failure," a piece that begins: "Mere reform won't fix policing." And activist Derecka Purnell's essay, "How I Became a Police Abolitionist." *Slate* columnist Joel Anderson wrote a piece on how cops condemning police brutality doesn't translate to anything real: "The Police Don't Change."

NBC News ran a cultural analysis of Kaba's book *We Do This 'Til We Free Us* called "Abolishing the Police Is A Lot More Practical Than Critics Claim." Some tried out more complicated positions, such as the idea that prisons should be abolished but kept for special exceptions: "I'm for Abolition. And Yet I Want the Capitol Rioters in Prison," read a headline in *The Nation*.

But the real tipping point was when glossy women's magazines came around to the cause. Abolition was hot. It was infinitely cooler than the alternative, the staid language of reform.

"What Is Abolition and Why Do We Need It?" abolition activists asked in *Vogue* magazine. *Vanity Fair* published anti-prison activist Josie Duffy Rice: "The promise of abolition is the promise of democracy itself."

From there it was everywhere. You could find a private nursery school in Berkeley releasing their pro-abolition statement ("Abolish the Police for the Safety of Our Community") along with annual tuition ($24,000 if possible, please).

Reform had been tried. Reform was the enemy. "Policing in our country is inherently & intentionally racist.... No more policing, incarceration and militarization. It can't be reformed," Congresswoman Rashida Tlaib wrote on Twitter.

If you had trouble imagining a police-free future, that was your problem, your lack of imagination, the limit of your creativity. Anything less than abolition is white supremacy. Rethink safety: property is just property. Rethink crime-fighting: Communities can care for each other. Crime largely exists because of poverty. Fix poverty, and there's no crime.

The replacement for police would be a whole system of social change. Without gentrification, maybe crime wouldn't happen. It would probably require the end of capitalism, though it could start with police funding going to therapy efforts, violence interrupters, and therapists, and self-defense training. For now, individuals should simply stop calling the police.

Muhammad Abdul-Ahad is a "violence interrupter" in Minneapolis. He and his coworkers walk their neighborhoods and intervene—interrupt—when something bad is happening or about to happen. When something looks a little sketchy or a fight's breaking out, the job is to physically interrupt it. Violence interrupters were not something I'd heard of before the last few years, when they became the central idea for those who want to eliminate police departments.

As for Muhammad, he oversees about twenty interrupters. They wear uniforms and carry walkie-talkies and flashlights—nothing else.

"We're not armed with guns but we are armed with a lot of training and a lot of experience and a lot of relationships," he told me when we talked. "Also a lot of love."

"It comes down to the relationship with the community. Respect comes both ways. We're not out there to tell people what not to do. We're able to walk up and hold conversations," he said. "Our message is to keep the peace."

He and his crew are a commanding presence.

"No one wants to pick up the phone and call 911. But there's still crime going on," Muhammad says. "We're out there to help prevent it. Hopefully our presence, us having a big group of twenty-plus men, our presence is intimidating enough. Looking like a football team. It's like, 'Wow, that'll give someone a second to think.'"

Sasha Cotton, then-director of the Office of Violence Prevention for Minneapolis, was running the program. The interrupters she chose develop relationships and use de-escalation.

"These are people who come from that lifestyle and know the players," Sasha said. "Sometimes it's as simple as putting someone in an Uber or taking them out for dinner."

Interrupter work is almost exclusively focused on gang violence and gun violence, and that usually starts out with little street scuffles between people—often teenagers and men in their early twenties—who know each other.

"People die over five-dollar bets," Sasha said. "People are shooting over what most of us would consider nonsensical issues: pride, perceived slights, you slept with my girlfriend."

Violence interrupters are accountable to their neighbors. People can retaliate if you cross a line, something that's harder to do with a police officer who doesn't live locally.

"If you manhandle somebody or treat them badly, then you are going to be worried about what they might do in retaliation," Sasha told me. "If you treat people with respect and with compassionate accountability, they're not likely to come back and do something to you and your family."

Muhammad said it takes courage to do this work. He doesn't have a gun. He doesn't wear a bulletproof vest.

When I ask about arming them or even giving them vests, Sasha balks.

"The bulletproof-vest model can create an environment that's counterintuitive," Sasha said. "We provide liability insurance and worker's comp, but this is different from policing."

"We never know what to expect, so we say our prayers," Muhammad told me. "Today I can go out there and run into five guys I've seen the night before. We have to go into it with some type of faith, some compassion to be out there to help these people. We're putting our lives out there daily not knowing what's going to happen. I've put myself into situations where I didn't know where it's going to end. Saving a life and changing a life, that's what success is."

Beginning in 2020, programs like Muhammad's expanded significantly. Congress approved $300 million in grants to community-based public safety efforts, and the Justice Department pledged $100 million in community violence reduction in late 2022. One major idea has been that police funding could be funneled instead into interrupter programs. Now there are dozens of these programs in cities around the country with thousands of new interrupters walking the streets and millions more in funding to expand further. There are violence-interrupter programs in New York and Los Angeles and Tucson and Houston.

Studies of these programs don't always show a reduction in

violence. Especially not for the interrupters themselves. But they feel right.

There were three killings of Safe Streets staffers in Baltimore between January 2021 and January 2022. Kenyell Wilson, a Safe Streets worker there, had been doing violence interruption work for nearly a decade when he was shot. He drove himself to the hospital, where he died. Dante Barksdale, another violence interrupter in Baltimore, was killed. In Southeast Washington, DC, Clarence Venable, who was still in training and was leaving a meeting for Cure the Streets, the local violence interruption program, when he was shot dead in 2019.

A few studies started coming out about what it was like to be an interrupter. One looked at violence interrupters in Chicago. It interviewed almost 200 of them, 87 percent of all community violence interventionists in the city. By and large, the authors found, interrupters are middle-aged black men. About 12 percent said they had been personally shot at over the last year on the job— more than one of them said a bullet actually hit them. About 20 percent have been "seriously threatened." For context: About 40 percent of big-city police officers report ever being shot at, and that's over their whole careers. Police have enormous legal protections, training, unions, pensions—not to mention guns.

So the trendiest progressive solution to violence was to disband police forces and then, instead, we would send groups of unarmed black men to defuse violent situations in our most dangerous neighborhoods. They wouldn't have a union. They wouldn't have pensions. They wouldn't have guns.

It sounded wild. It sounded pie in the sky. But cities actually passed resolutions to defund or, in some cases, abolish their police departments. It was all really happening.

New York City then-mayor Bill de Blasio wanted to shift $1 billion of funding out of the police budget, saying, "We think it's the right thing to do." It would be invested into youth services: "Our young people need to be reached, not policed," the mayor said. The city council approved that budget 32–17. New York's plainclothes anticrime unit's focus on gun violence was temporarily disbanded in 2020. (It was renamed and brought back two years later, and the police budget was increased by some $200 million.)

Keisha Lance Bottoms, then Atlanta's mayor, said that "defunding the police" was about reallocating funding to social services and community initiatives, and added, "We've been doing this work over the last couple of years." (Atlanta did not end up defunding their department.)

Baltimore City Council president at the time and now the city's mayor, Brandon Scott, said he was "proud to lead a City Council that took the first step to responsibly reduce Baltimore's budget dependence on policing," as the council approved a new $22 million cut to the police budgets. (The next year, they walked it back.)

"The department is irredeemably beyond reform," wrote then-Minneapolis City Council member Steve Fletcher, who then joined eight other council members on a stage draped with a giant banner that read: DEFUND POLICE. The city council unanimously approved a proposal to abolish the police force or,

WE MEAN, LITERALLY, ABOLISH THE POLICE

technically, "to change the city charter to allow the police department to be dismantled."

San Francisco's mayor came out in favor of defunding and passed plans to cut $120 million from the police budget. (These plans actually never materialized, and SF's police budget continued to grow.) Portland, Oregon, did cut $15 million—and then agreed to use general funding to hire new police officers.

"Please take a moment to celebrate this victory and let it fuel your fire, because we're not done," said one of the Portland city commissioners. "We're not done."

In Austin, Texas, police announced that, due to staffing shortages and in line with the city's "Reimagining Public Safety" program, they would stop responding to "non-emergencies," and that citizens should report things that had "no immediate threat to life or property" by calling 311 rather than 911.

There were numbers showing considerable support given how radical the idea seemed: 27 percent of Oregonians supported abolishing the police, according to one June 2021 poll. Among those under 30, a full 45 percent supported eliminating the police department.

But some of the polling didn't look as clean. It was confusing. It looked almost as though black Americans wanted police departments.

A study from the University of Michigan found that in Detroit, white residents were nearly twice as likely as black residents to say that an increased police presence in their neighborhoods would make them feel less safe. White supremacy mindset, no doubt. New Detroit residents were three times as likely as longtime residents to say they would feel unsafe with an increased police presence.

By October 2021, only 23 percent of black Americans wanted police funding cut in their area, according to Pew Research.

Before terms like *defund* and *abolish* crash into our Instagram feeds as memes, they begin as ideas at places like Columbia Law School.

Bernard E. Harcourt is developing a model curriculum there called Abolition Democracy and has taught courses like, Abolition: A Social Justice Practicum. He also gives lectures on the topic. He is the Isidor and Seville Sulzbacher Professor of Law, a professor of political science, and founding director of the Initiative for a Just Society at the Columbia Center for Contemporary Critical Thought at Columbia University—and a directeur d'études at the École des Hautes Études en Sciences Sociales in Paris.

For his 2020 event—Abolition: Abolish the Police—he has brought together a number of police abolitionists, including Amna Akbar, a law professor at Ohio State University.

"Policing and criminal law enforcement were and are today what I've come to call the linchpin in the new mechanisms post-slavery to recreate a racial hierarchy in this country," Harcourt says, citing police collaborating with the Ku Klux Klan for lynchings, for example. "Never before in American history has the call to defund and abolish the police resonated so loudly across the country. It has turned police abolition into almost a mainstream idea."

Akbar launches into a sort of spoken-word academic poetry

about what abolition means, what it looks like, what it feels like, what it's connected to:

> Abolition is not just about undoing, it is about doing . . . abolition is not just about burning, it is about assembling. . . . It's not just about saying prisons and police are racist, classist, misogynist, death-dealing institutions; it's about asking what institutions we might build.
>
> We're living in a time where we're seeing all sorts of grassroots demands—to abolish prisons and police, yes, but also to abolish rent, debt, borders, billionaires, to decommodify housing and healthcare, to decolonize land.

Bernard thanks her.

The goal of abolition—here is lawyer, writer, and organizer Derecka Purnell—is "not so much the abolition of prisons, but the abolition of a society that could have prisons. That could have slavery. That could have the wage. And therefore, not abolition as the elimination of anything, but abolition as the founding of a new society."

Bernard likes that. "Thank you for posing both the historical embeddedness and the theoretical embeddedness to understand the resistance, also, within a framework, as you yourself suggested, of abolition democracy."

So that's the theory. But what about the practice? What about people who say it's too hard to abolish the police?

Josmar Trujillo, a writer and abolition organizer, says police will be obsolete.

"There was a time when no one could imagine that we could have medicine without blood-sucking leeches," Trujillo says. "There was a time when no one could see a society where we didn't have kings and queens."

And violence? How will violence be handled?

Well. Everyone on the panel is in agreement: violence almost always has a reason. Someone is violent because they have been hurt or impoverished. Eliminate poverty and pain, and then violence won't be an issue.

Believing in police means you believe that people will always hurt each other, that people will always steal from one another. The abolitionist asks: What if that's not true? What if human nature can be good? What if the crimes happen because we believe the crimes will happen?

"Doubting the possibility that we can get rid of police is accepting that harm is a constant," says Ghislaine Pagès, former executive coordinator for the Columbia Center for Contemporary Critical Thought. "If we weren't learning violence from the government and if we weren't having violence done, the violence of poverty, the violence of racism done onto people, what would harm look like? We just don't know."

■

When the crime wave came—and it did—it baffled leaders. In blue cities, crime spiked to levels not seen in decades. Philadelphia's murder rate in 2021 and 2022 was the highest it had been in sixty-three years. Los Angeles's homicides reached a fifteen-year high. In 2023, Seattle saw the most homicides it had in forty-four years. "If there are solutions that we have not explored and enacted, I welcome the suggestions," said then Atlanta mayor Bottoms in December 2020, after a seven-year-old was killed. Atlanta city councilman Antonio Brown, who voted to defund the police in 2020, had his car stolen by mid-2021. Armed robbers held up a news crew as it interviewed Oakland's chief of violence prevention in mid-2021. The entire Portland police riot squad resigned that year too. More than a dozen gunshots rang out during a newscast from George Floyd Square.

A conflict played out in West Oakland in the summer of 2021 about how to address these ideas about violence and policing.

A group of black families and activists—about two hundred or so people—were holding a memorial for seventy-one homicide victims. It was seen as a police friendly event, and representatives from the Oakland Police Department were there. Organizers were going to read the names of the people killed recently in their community. The hope was to memorialize the dead and also to rally around support for public safety efforts. The Oakland City Council had just decided to cut the police department budget by $18 million.

They had a small platform in the park for speakers. "When I thought about what I would say to you today, I had to reflect on what someone asked me before this event: Is this the one with the boring speeches or is this the one with the food and the music?" said Carol Wyatt, who has served on the Oakland Community Policing Advisory Board and the Reimagining Public Safety

Task Force. "I said, 'The one with the speeches 'cause dead people don't eat Twinkies or listen to music.'"

"No matter our station in the black community we cannot move past the burials, the memorial," Wyatt said. "The wakes bring us all together."

As she spoke, another group started to form near the rally of older black residents. It was a counter-protest: "The Anti Police-Terror Project's Reimagine Safety Community Celebration & Caravan"—or "the ACAB protestors," as Wyatt later called them.

The promotional materials for the counterprotest featured images of black people but the protester group was almost entirely white, a small but loud group of maybe a dozen or two. One counter-protestor was wearing a hat with the image of a rifle and the word *Equality*. They were shouting and holding signs: FUCK OPD, ACAB, CARE NOT CAGES.

"They're using your pain as a shield!" one of them shouted toward the crowd of black families.

A write-up of the event by one of the counter-protestors on a left-wing website described the black families present as "Nazis." It described them as using "right-wing extremist" tactics.

While family members of those killed spoke, the counter-protestors screamed. They held a sign that read *Police are domestic terrorists*. They spoke over the rally on a bullhorn. They chanted.

The black families and community activists displayed a coffin and seventy-one white flowers, each one representing a person killed recently in Oakland. Each victim's name was read out loud while the counter-protestors read names of people killed by police to drown it out.

A middle school teacher talked about how the violence in his neighborhood has hurt his students. The former police chief, LeRonne Armstrong, spoke.

"The people in the hills live a really good life but the people in East Oakland live a different life," Armstrong said. "Their voices need to be heard. You need to hear from the people in East Oakland. You need to see the trauma that they are experiencing every day."

Inevitably, there was a confrontation. Some of the community activists ended up confronting the ring of counter-protestors, trying to get them to be quiet. It was all caught on video.

An older black woman wearing a sun hat and a T-shirt memorializing a missing teenager approached the protesters, some friends in tow.

"White privilege is standing here. You think you have a right to be here," she said, tension in her voice as it got louder. "You don't have a right to be here."

The woman next to her, wearing a #SafeOakland shirt, added: "Not when black children are dying in the street every day . . ."

"Yeah, at the hands of the police," one of the ACAB protestors said.

"NO!" the black woman yelled back, frustrated.

Backing her up was an athletic-looking man with a thick beard: "What do you have against safety in Oakland? Why do you try to disrupt something that's positive? We're trying to save our people. You are not our people. Get the fuck out."

The tension escalated. Many of the ACAB protestors had covered their faces in the fashion of these protestors. "Let me see your face, let me see your face," one man there for the rally yelled. "You take that shit somewhere else, this is a motherfucking memorial. This is a memorial, man. Don't be disrespectful."

"The presence of the cops is disrespectful," the ACAB protester said back to him. "They're using your pain as a shield."

Some of the ACAB kids started to laugh. They'd gotten everyone's goat.

The black families started giving up. "The fuck you talking about," one man said to a petite white person with purple hair.

Guns became the number-one cause of child death in America, since surpassing car accidents in 2020. The number of murders in America rose by almost 30 percent in 2020. It was the largest single-year increase in the American homicide rate in at least a century, maybe ever. But #Defund activists stayed the course anyway. Some of them had to make adjustments to their own lives. US representative Jamaal Bowman, who is pro-defunding, requested special police protection for his Yonkers home after January 6.

Congresswoman Cori Bush is, on the one hand, pushing hard to defund the police. On the other hand, she spent $70,000 on private security over just a few months, much more than the average for a congresswoman. She was asked about any complexity in pushing to defund while spending that much.

"You would rather me die? Is that what you want to see? You want to see me die? You know, because that could be the alternative. So either I spent $70,000 on private security over the last few months, and I'm here standing now and able to speak, able to help save 11 million people from being evicted," she said to CBS News. "So suck it up—and defunding the police has to happen. We need to defund the police and put that money into social safety nets because we're trying to save lives."

The idea that policing only hurts people became embedded in the culture. In Brooklyn one day in 2022, a man with a large stick attacked a woman and her dog. The dog, a golden retriever mix named Moose, died from his injuries. But the man, a park regular, remained free. For months, the police did nothing— even when the woman spied the attacker again, calling the police ten times as she pursued him.

A small neighborhood-watch group formed. But it quickly fell apart after its first and only meeting. The watch group is white supremacy, and protestors crashed it to criticize them for involving police. A tree now grows in the park for Moose.

What should she have done to abide by this philosophy? The only acceptable thing for that woman with that golden retriever to do would have been to also have a stick and to fight back right then and there. She should have been training for the moment.

The attacker is also a victim, a local elected official explained. The homeless man with the stick is a victim too, the elected kept saying. The woman, allowing her dog to be attacked, victimizing the man.

I take this to heart. To be victimized by crime is to victimize the one committing the crime. The responsible anti-racist thing to do is not to run and call the cops. It's to fight back in the moment. That's your option. So when the man comes with a stick to kill our dumb little shelter dogs, I have to have a stick to fight back. To defend yourself in the moment is the only anti-racist response. The real white supremacy is *not* buying a gun.

Part III

MEN AND NON-MEN

Wi Spa

Wi Spa billed itself as "a convenient and affordable place to de-stress and be pampered," but one summer week in 2021 it became a site of great stress because of one (allegedly, partially) erect penis that had manifested in the women's room.

The spa, in Los Angeles's Koreatown, has separate men's and women's areas where people go naked. The penis went bobbing through the women's space. The penis had been seen soaking in the women's communal soak pools. Women enjoying their spa time were upset. One went to the front desk asking for help, saying there were children present and that there was a man in the bathroom. The front desk could not help. The person with the penis had a California driver's license that listed their gen-der as "female." The penis was white, and some of the women who didn't want to see it were black Hispanic, which in the sum-mer of 2021 might have helped draw knee-jerk public sympathy, but apparently did not.

Someone started recording a video of the woman complain-ing at the front desk. It went online, and it went viral.

She later held a press conference with a lawyer, and protests starting springing up. Seeing that the spa needed to be defended, trans activists gathered. They would defend the spa and defend all trans people, now represented by the spa.

"ROUND TWO MOTHERFUCKERS SMASH TRANSPHO-BIA SMASH FASCISM," read the invitation on social media.

The transition from Black Lives Matter to Trans Lives Matter was seamless. It hardly warranted notice. As Black Lives Matter faltered, as #AbolishThePolice lost its luster in the murders and the chaos and the vast missing funds, there was no pause. I don't think this was planned or orchestrated. The movement simply pivoted: The conversation about racism was now about trans-phobia. Done! Go!

The morning of the protest, technically guarding but also blocking the doors to the spa, the Los Angeles Police Depart-ment deployed itself. Like a candy-coating shell, a hundred or so pro-trans protestors surrounded the cops. A handful of conser-vatives gathered in a pocket a block away to also defend the spa but differently and for some reason seemed content to rally among each other.

The trans activists were having fun. Their in-house band

played on the sidewalk. It was a warm, sunny day, and it smelled like LA, a little acidic, a little like grilled meat. Someone in a bright-pink blow-up unicorn suit danced in the streets. They waved the gay Antifa flag—a rainbow flag with a rifle across it. Unfortunately there were no visible transphobes present to yell at around Wi Spa, so the agenda for the day became trans activists v. police.

At the front of the spa defense scrum was a woman in tight green shorts and a crop top. She wore her hair in two little buns and she was vibrating with rage. "You're disgusting," she seethed at the cops. "You're short and disgusting. I don't sleep with short men." The penis and its right to be in that spa, erect or otherwise, barely came up.

Her compatriots—almost all of ambiguous gender presentation, though Green Shorts's pronouns were she/her, because she shouted them—chimed in, screaming at the mostly black and Latino officers: "You'll never be white. You think you're white but you're not."

One hefty man with a bandana around his face and a handheld microphone attached to his phone for live-streaming went on a tear for his streaming audience's delight. "Fuck this bitch pig motherfucker fuck this bitch fuck this bitch. Wait till the armed people come out here one day and we outnumber y'all and we out gun y'all?"

The person in the blow-up pink unicorn outfit ended a break-dance routine and began calmly live-streaming as well. The *LA Times*, they said, "is getting people to vilify protestors." A pretty young woman in a pressed white button-front and slacks and a *New Yorker* bag was throwing hand signs for pictures; a woman in pink hair was at a drum set making the background music for it all.

Across the street was a clutch of Antifa who looked less festive. Their faces were entirely covered; most were in tactical vests and goggles. They were holding umbrellas—and they were watching me.

These protesters had been gathering for a while, roving to different sites of American gender fascism, and so I was quickly clocked as a newcomer. *I haven't seen you at these before*, someone said to me.

It was a lovely day. The cops were pretty relaxed at this point. It was hard not to dance along to the drums. Several protestors were swaying in the street, casually blocking traffic. Green Shorts had taken a break. "Does anybody need Gatorade? Snacks? Goldfish?"

Someone walked by with a skateboard. "Any camera I need to block, let me know, let me know!"

The jeers at the police become more specific.

At a female cop: "As a woman upholding the sexist fucking patriarchy they don't care about you. You're protecting homophobic white supremacist transphobia."

At a male officer: "You have a tiny no-dick. We're going to show this video to your family so they know."

To a black officer: "Black cops showing up for white cops. They don't give a shit about you, bro. You'll be the first one they throw under the bus."

To an officer I assume is named Brad: "You don't have the balls to kill yourself. Kill yourself, Brad. You're a waste of the planet. You know you've been thinking about it a long time. Kill yourself, Brad, do it! You're a piece of shit. I'm gonna start following you around till you kill yourself."

My new friend Green Shorts was especially animated during the taunting, saying to a female officer: "Fuck all of you, especially this white bitch right here. You stupid bitch. We hate you. Eat a dick. Sit on a cactus. Bitch." Green Shorts was cooling off with a paper fan as she turned to the men: "You're a pussy ass bitch and you're all shorter than me. I'm sorry, I don't date short guys. You beat your wife and your children; that's why your wife is cheating on you." She paused, fanned, and took a breath. "You short fucks."

Then I noticed that something was off. The pretty girl in the pressed slacks was taking my picture. Umbrellas were unfurled to block my view. I realized they were screaming at me. They were live-streaming me.

They were screaming: "Tomas, Tomas, you know you'll never be white, Tomas." I looked at the man to my right. This had to be Tomas. He shrugged as if to say sorry about all this. We'd been chatting.

A braver person would defend this Tomas, who seemed harmless enough, but I put my hands in the air. "I don't know him, I don't know Tomas," I said. "Tomas who?" I scurried away to the side and laughed. "I've never met Tomas," I told Green Shorts and whoever else would listen.

As the group circled him, police came to escort him down the block. Tomas turns out to be Tomas Morales, a conservative Latino videographer. "I'll find you next time, Tomas. You won't make it out, I promise you that. Come back, Tomas!" someone yelled. I was in the screaming group, my phone held high to capture the scene, just like everyone else.

I realized only then that I probably shouldn't have worn so much black.

Two ladies, one older, one younger, were trying to get through the crowd in a car. They didn't look like they were here for a counterprotest, but maybe they were. Protestors started screaming at them, *Nazis! Yeah, fuck you.* The cameras turned to them; they were terrified, the older one white-knuckling her steering wheel.

Nearby, a small guy in a black ski mask was pointing a bright flashlight at a tall masked man. They were in a fight.

"The indigenous tribes were anarchists," the small guy yells.

Green Shorts wanted to know why the tall guy was there. She suspected he was not with the movement. No one other than allies are allowed to record protests. This is a law of this sort of protest. Groups train new members how to block cameras and how to snatch and smash them. She was asking him if he supports trans rights. He was trying to ignore her, but soon they were in an argument. It turned out he wasn't an anarchist, and he thought it was all kind of dumb.

"There should be no private property," Green Shorts said, and started lecturing him about his "ancestors."

"Why are you assuming my heritage?" he asked. "I have Cherokee heritage."

"I'm half Navajo Mexicana," she said. "You have to decolonize your mind. Your Cherokee ancestors are extremely disappointed in you. If you want some sort of government, let the indigenous tribes take care of the land like they were for thousands of years before colonizers came over here—the real savages. Native Americans, we traveled, we walked. We did not just go out and murder and pillage."

"The Native American tribes of North America were genociding each other," he said.

"No, no they weren't," she said. "That's where you're really fucked up. You're a fucking idiot. I've been out at every single protest, and I haven't seen you. I don't have to be peaceful. I don't owe anybody peace. Do you support trans people? I'm asking you a question. I identify as both female and trans and nonbinary. I am a biological pussy-having person—OK, I have a uterus. Transphobe piece of shit. We have a transphobe over here!"

Help arrived in the form of a man wielding a skateboard and a man in a purple wig. They shoved the tall guy with the board. The tall guy was upset because he said he was maced by these guys before. Purple Wig disagreed: "Nobody maced you, you fucking bitch. It's not mace. It's not mace. Hairspray is not mace. You're pretty lucky you haven't gotten your shit whacked yet."

A crowd gathered to chant at the tall man. "Get out, get out, get out, get out of here, get out."

But he just stayed there.

Eventually people get bored of shoving him, and the police

were right there, so they moved away. But Green Shorts stayed. It goes on so long between them, yelling for the sake of the livestreams.

They argued about trans athletes in the Olympics, steroid usage, whether or not Native Americans went to war with each other, and whether Native Americans all had matrilineal antiracist societies. They went over specific books each had read or not read.

Eventually, focus returned to the protest when someone pulled out a switchblade. A police officer noticed, and the man immediately dropped the knife to the ground by my feet. "There was no knife," protestors shouted, as I edged away from the knife. "There was no knife!"

Green Shorts shimmied, all wrapped up in a trans rights flag. Young families propped open building grates to watch the commotion. Older Chinese women in visors power walked past. A black teenager smoking a cigarette asked what's going on. Three white men responded, almost in unison, that they were defending the spa. "Oh," he said. "OK."

After the protest, some journalists and activists wrote that the whole thing—the penis in the women's spa—was a right-wing hoax to stir up trouble. *The Guardian* called it "misinformation" and *Slate* called it "an alleged transphobic hoax." The trans woman, one version goes, was actually a straight man there to antagonize everyone against trans people. And the woman complaining to the front desk? She was in on it too, a fake. We needed to Believe Women except not these women, not about that.

The facts always take a while to come clear. In this case, it took a while for it all to rattle out. More than a year later, Darren Merager, a middle-aged registered sex offender with a history of indecent exposure, was arrested for indeed being in the women's section of the spa, bringing a penis along. Four women and a girl went to the police about it. Going into women's spaces and exposing that penis seems to be Darren's thing. Darren had done it in a West Hollywood women's bathroom just a bit earlier. What would Wi Spa do when Darren showed up with an ID, on which it said *Sex: Female*? (In California, you can change your sex on a driver's license without a court order or medical certificate.) They would let Darren in to roam the women's floor. Still, Darren was charged with five felony counts of indecent exposure. The crux of the case rests on Darren's intent. And the crux of intent rests on that penis. Was it hard?

On a chilly winter day in 2023, Darren showed up to a big modern courthouse, near LAX. That day Darren was actually facing two hearings in the same building: In one room, Darren was representing herself in a case alleging indecent exposure in a West Hollywood women's changing area back in 2018. In one room, Darren was choosing to be referred to as a woman. In the other, Darren was actually going as a man. Or at least this is what he told me.

I sat next to Darren in the Wi Spa hearing, where Darren is going as *he*, and we started to chat. He was wearing loose, drapey clothes over his lanky frame. He's soft-spoken and has a gentleness to him, his fine brown hair combed nicely, his hands resting on his lap. He carries a big binder with him. Darren's stepdad came, a little late, sighing about traffic. Darren couldn't believe all the protests.

"I'm as surprised as you are," he told me.

Darren had actually been at the Wi Spa rally, sitting in a car, watching it all. Protestors even came to yell at him, accusing him of being a white supremacist. "They thought I was a Proud Boy."

"Probably because of my hair," he said, feeling it for a moment. "They tried to attack me."

He was upset that people thought it was a hoax. He'd definitely been in the spa. He'd actually spent the night there.

Court came into session. The prosecutors had one argument to make: Darren's penis had been hard. The prosecution: "Was his penis soft or was it hard?" The defense carefully cross-examined to prove that it had, in fact, been soft. The defense: "And when you saw the person's penis as the person walked, was the penis hard or was it soft?"

One of the witnesses had trouble answering. She was fourteen years old. It was the first penis she'd ever seen.

Asexual Awareness
Month / The End of Sex

Michaela Kennedy-Cuomo is an American princess, or as close to it as our country can make. Her mother is a Kennedy, and Michaela has that family's beauty. Her father is Andrew Cuomo, the longtime governor of New York, son of the former governor of New York, and she has the Cuomo family's great sense of stagecraft.

So it made international news when Michaela Kennedy-Cuomo stood in front of a rainbow flag and came out as queer during June 2021—Pride Month, of course.

"Today, I stand in my queer identity with pride, and in memory of those who came before me. I stand indebted to the activists who fought for my right to love and happiness. I stand with a helping hand outreached to those finding their way from under socially constructed boxes to emerge from the closet. I'm standing with you," she said.

This was overshadowed by her father's resignation as governor of New York two months later (he was accused of sexual harassment and misconduct) and her uncle's firing as a CNN anchor six months later (he was accused of improperly helping his brother), but here she was: She was coming out. She was queer.

Actually, she later clarified, she was coming out as asexual-adjacent. Specifically: demisexual.

"To those who are contending with the compulsive hetero-sexuality our society force feeds us and innate attraction beyond cis het folks," Michaela said, meaning people who had hetero-sexual relationships with people living as the genders they were born into, "please know that you are not alone."

Demisexuals identify as part of the asexual spectrum. The asexuals, who sometimes go by *ace*, are one of the newer members of the alphabet soup of modern pan-gay identity (LGBTQIA+). There is an asexual flag: a black stripe for asexuality, gray for the in-between, white for sex (or lack of), and purple for community.

Within the asexual cluster you will find the demisexuals. Their type of asexuality is that they are not attracted to strangers. A demisexual is attracted to another person *only* after a strong emotional bond has been established. That bond could be a friendship or a date. A demisexual might have a quite typical sex life.

But it can now feel fraught for the demisexual person. The largest source of international LGBTQ+ news, *PinkNews*, ran an article about it: "Demisexual gay trans man says his asexuality was 'the hardest label to define.'"

Within the wheel of asexuality, demisexual sits in contrast with the "fraysexual." That's someone who largely experiences sexual attraction toward people they don't know. The attraction fades away after they get to know the person.

So Michaela threw a coming-out party to tell the world that she wanted to date only people she liked. A few weeks later, she held a public conversation for Pride Month with Donato Tramuto, the former CEO of Tivity Health, which provides health-related employee perks.

"When I was in elementary school, I feared that I was lesbian," Michaela said. "When I was in middle school, I came out to my family and close friends as bisexual. When I was in high school, I discovered pansexuality and thought, 'That's the flag for me.' I've recently learned more about demisexuality and have believed that that identity resonates with me most."

The more people talked about sex and tried to create ever more elaborate labels to exactly describe their sexual proclivities, it seemed the less sex most Americans were having. Let alone having children. There's something too personal and indulgent about all that.

All over the country, people are having less sex, fewer children, and fewer marriages. We're all asexuals now.

One night in Los Angeles's Eastside, I was at dinner with half a dozen friends of mine from college—midthirties handsome, successful, great guys. There was a professor, a lawyer, an artist. We were sitting in the backyard after dinner. The boys were smoking cigars. And the topic turned to kids. No one seemed to want them.

A PEW survey in 2021 found that among non-parents younger than fifty, the majority say they "just don't want to have children." A smaller group have more specific reasons, like cost or the environment.

It's immoral, a friend told me. The damage one child does to the environment? If you were someone who never recycled and who drove a Hummer, that still wouldn't be as bad for the environment as bringing another human life to the party. Then there's the obvious reality that the climate apocalypse is around the corner, they say. There is no stopping it, why reproduce? In a couple generations, your descendants will probably die anyway. Plus, with America going to hell, how could you bring new life into this?

(A few days after that dinner, *The Washington Post* had an article about a new climate-change-awareness beer: "There's nothing quite like a cold beer to finish a long work week. Unless, of course, that beer reminds you of suffocating heat waves, explosive wildfires, mega-droughts, devastating floods, or their risks to human health and the environment.")

The only dissent that night was from a date, a young woman down at the far end of a bench. She was from the South, just visiting. She wants kids, she said. I never saw her again.

Fertility rates have been on the decline since 2007, and, since 2014, births in the United States have declined 2 percent every year. Then the birth rate dropped 4 percent during the early stages of the Covid-19 pandemic in 2020—with just a 1 percent slight bounce back from that low level in 2021.

Or another way to measure it: In 1990, an average group of one thousand women in their childbearing years would birth about seventy children, according to the US Census. By 2019, it was around fifty-six children.

Americans are also having much less sex than they used to. That's a trend that's been going on for years now, long before the pandemic, but nothing seems to be stopping it. According to the General Social Survey, about one in four adults didn't have sex at all in 2018, one survey found. And according to a report by the National Center for Health Statistics, the US marriage rate keeps hitting new all-time lows.

Nearly one third of young men under thirty say they've never had sex with a woman since turning eighteen, according to a study by Indiana University researchers. That number was fewer than one in ten back in 2008. Babies? They're out. Sex? We can take it or leave it. An essay published in *Outside* magazine on a handsome young man getting a vasectomy for climate change had been making the rounds and getting accolades.

The first time I heard about the asexual revolution was at The New York Times. Not in the paper, but at the paper. In the fall of 2020, I got an alert: it was asexuality celebration time at The

New York Times—and there was a week of programming to go along with it.

There would be a panel for staff and employees: "Reclaiming the A in LGBTQIA+." And then, "to continue our observance of Ace Week," the paper also offered an asexual reading and book club session for Timeseans later in the week. (The book: "A breathtaking debut novel featuring an asexual, Apache teen protagonist, 'Elatsoe,' combines mystery, horror, noir, ancestral knowledge, haunting illustrations, fantasy elements, and is one of the most-talked about debuts of the year.")

The asexual week panel, held as a large video call, was packed with seven speakers and an audience of reporters and newsroom leaders. We were all there to learn how best to cover it.

First the question was how exactly to define the asexuals. It started easy enough.

"*Asexual* people experience little to no sexual attraction. We rarely, if ever, see someone and feel sexually attracted to them," said Elizabeth, the head of a New York City asexuality group, defining the terminology.

But it's not quite so simple. Because while attraction can be absent, libidinous desire can still be very present for an asexual.

"Your libido can be high, but you can still be asexual because it could just be that you are physically turned on," Elizabeth explains. "But that isn't directed at anyone. It's just the body is like, 'I am turned on right now,' and you're like, 'OK. Not going to do anything with that.'

"*Desire* is more of a conscious decision. Desire is you want to have sex with someone. It is more of a conscious choice. So an asexual person could desire to have sex with someone because they think sex feels good or they would like to have biological children, so they may have sexual *desire* for someone while not being sexually *attracted* to them. This can get complicated and this is kind of getting into the asexuality 201 / 301 levels."

Many of the asexuals discovered other folks like them. That's how another panelist found the term *graysexual*, which worked for them for a while. Graysexual is a handy bucket category of people who range along a spectrum of being repulsed by or only mildly interested in sex. (I'm also losing track here.)

Sarah Costello, who cohosts an asexual-oriented podcast, discovered asexuality on Tumblr in high school, then in college returned to those Tumblrs.

"I went back and did some more research and came to the realization that I was both aromantic and asexual."

Nailing down these labels—the titles of each identity—seemed very important. Many involved with the asexual community describe spending years exploring the different labels, trying on several different ones, feeling right with a label—and then suddenly wrong with it, needing a new one. The process of discovering sexuality or lack thereof is in part a linguistic journey. Bodies are ambiguous and messy, with desires that pop up and disappear, and there's something comforting in a tight, contained label. Also the more niche the label, the smaller and more tight-knit the community. There's pleasure in finding that community. Sexuality is explored less with other bodies and more by visiting these communities online.

"Every queer kid has this phase where they're on the internet and Googling all the vocabulary, just trying to figure out what's going on with them," another panelist said. (My coming out involved fellow teens more than Google, but times have changed.)

Also on the call was Kayla Kaszyca, Sarah's cohost. Both were then fresh out of college. The podcast is called *Sounds Fake But Okay*. That's a common way people respond when an asexual explains their orientation.

As podcast hosts, Kayla was supposed to be the fun straight-girl foil to Sarah, an outspoken aromantic asexual. Podcast episodes would have Sarah asking questions like, "Why do people kiss?" and "What's dating like?"

But the premise fell apart the longer they talked.

"I slowly realized through the first couple of episodes that, 'Oh, no, I'm also on the asexual spectrum,'" she said. Kayla now identifies as a bi-demisexual, and so is part of the queer community: "It means that I only experience sexual attraction when I have this strong kind of emotional or romantic connection to someone."

She said that now, in a heterosexual relationship, demisexuality wasn't so much of an issue.

But when she was dating: "I had to continually come out to people that I'm not going to have sex with them on the first date or whatever," she said. But again, now there's the boyfriend. "I guess the only reason it impacts my life a ton right now is because of the podcast."

Sarah and Kayla would go on to write a fun self-help book about using the asexual mindset in life and love. This can be useful in moments such as telling a guy you're not having sex on the first date.

They all find it frustrating the "the queer community" won't completely accept them.

"There's a lot of gatekeeping of saying Aces aren't oppressed enough to be queer, which, A, that isn't the point of the queer community, and, B, yes, we are if we really want to fight about it like that," Kayla said.

Sarah added: "In queer communities, a lot of times what we get is, 'I acknowledge that the way you feel is valid, but I don't think you belong in this community.' Being a member, being a part of the queer community is not supposed to be the oppression Olympics."

Asexuals also hope that those who aren't asexual start to take on a special name. Those we used to not exactly have a name for—sexual-attraction-level-normal?—are now named *allosexual* or *zedsexual*. Just as *cisgender* is used to describe those who aren't trans, non-asexuals should begin to identify as such. As in, I, Nellie, am an allosexual. A man who likes women? That's a cis-het-allo.

As the Tumblr-inspired identities have proliferated, and as the "LGTBQIA+ community" has grown to include America's Kaylas and Sarahs and Michaelas, that world of gays and lesbians became somewhat old-fashioned. Almost quaint.

Now, of course, it's a wonderful thing to be so popular that many would-be straight people want to join.

But when Supreme Court justice Clarence Thomas writes, in the decision overturning the right to abortion at the federal level, that "we should reconsider all of this Court's substantive due process precedents," which means for both contraception and gay marriage, you might get nervous that focus is drifting from some key elements.

Lesbians of a certain age (I probably fit that demographic at this point) are the most radical on all this, annoyed that all these trendy kids are confusing the whole project. How am I meant to caucus with a girl who is dating a boy but considers herself queer because they waited to have sex? When did all these new people start calling themselves LGBTQIA+? Why do they want this? How many places higher up the progressive stack does it even take them? My favorite radical feminist, Julie Bindel, one of the leaders of England's old-school feminist movement, likened the new community name to a Wi-Fi password. Bindel and some other radical feminists (as they've taken to calling themselves) put together a new nonprofit—The Lesbian Project—and launched in 2023. From their manifesto: "The Lesbian Project works to build a knowledge base about lesbian lives, promote sensible and evidence-based policy, and contribute to building lesbian community in the UK and internationally." The project excludes trans women (biological males) who are attracted to women, and the activists who represent that group get very upset about being excluded from any female spaces but most of all lesbian spaces. And so The Lesbian Project is today considered a form of hate speech.

Gay rights were largely won by making homosexuality seem

apolitical—*born this way* was the mantra. Gays were just like you. A lot of gay men had to put on ill-fitting khakis and stand for photos by white picket fences before gay marriage could go from absurd to the law of the land.

But that is not what the new members want.

For the new members, being in the community means, more than anything else, that they hate those white picket fences.

There is a sense that to be queer is mystical and maybe holy. The Long Now Foundation, a group that puts together events to encourage future-thinking and whose efforts are in part funded by Jeff Bezos, held an event in 2021 called, "Queering the Future: How LGBTQ Foresight Can Benefit All."

And so all America's smart elites are queer. The term now indicates a worldview. An essay by a woman in a relationship with a man went viral in May 2021: "My straight boyfriend gave me a queer pandemic haircut—as he sawed through my thick mane, we invited queerness into the bathroom—and into our relationship."

Queerness is an aesthetic and a politics. It's a culture, a rebellion. The only thing queerness has little to do with is sex. To base gayness in something like physical arousal is appalling to the new movement. The body has very little to do with all of this. And that's good, the movement tells us. The body and sex are suspect. It's fitting that *asexual* would become one of the more popular new labels.

The new asexuals aren't a unique feature of the Left. There's a similar rise on the right. Some of these men identify as incels, an abbreviation of the term *involuntary celibate*, the idea being that because of feminism no one wants to have sex with them.

There's one group in particular I've become obsessed with—they call themselves MGTOW, Men Going Their Own Way. They're fascinated with the idea that modern life is intent on emasculating them. Part of their proof: How radically sperm counts are falling in industrialized nations. Which is a real thing.

A book came out called *Count Down: How Our Modern World Is Threatening Sperm Counts, Altering Male and Female Reproductive Development, and Imperiling the Future of the Human Race*. It was written by Shanna Swan, a professor at the Icahn School of Medicine at Mount Sinai in New York City. Academia was not happy about it.

I got a press release from Harvard's GenderSci Lab, which argues we should not talk about "sperm decline" at all. Sure, it's happening. But one should just talk about it as new variability. Framing it as a problem is racist and sexist:

> Among the reasons to consider alternative interpretations of sperm count patterns than that of precipitous and fertility-threatening declines in men's sperm counts is the life of such theories in Alt-Right, white supremacist, and men's rights discourse. These groups have used Swan's research to argue that the fertility and health of men in whiter nations are in imminent danger, often linking the danger to the perceived increase in ethnic and racial diversity and to the influence of feminist and anti-racist social movements.

Men's rights discourse. In the new asexual America, it's not just adorable straight women. There are also men. And whatever falling sperm counts means, it feels like something bad. And some men are feeling disoriented. Or angry.

I signed up to go see about those men.

The conference was called Make Women Great Again. Several of the leaders and speakers were major voices in the manosphere—the loose collection of men's rights blogs and conferences. One invited me to come out for the event, so I flew to Orlando. He told me to come to a cigar bar one night to meet the group. There was some confusion when I showed up. The man who invited me pretended not to know me. He was sitting with the men's rights crew and when I got there, he avoided eye contact, giving me an odd soft, limp handshake. He didn't tell his friends I'd be coming. He later admonished me—I should have waited on the corner, he said. But there I was in an Orlando cigar bar. A reporter! A spy! A female! The guys started livestreaming me to their social media channels. I tried my best to smile and apologize for the chaos. I was glad I wore a nice silk blouse for my close-up. I headed back to the hotel and flew out the next morning, more confused than anything.

They spent more than a year afterward making videos about me, obsessing over every scrap of text and video from that night, annotating screenshots. The conference host would post updates that began, "My fellow manospherians." Oddly, they invited me back.

For some reason, I did go back. Instead of attending an Indigo Girls concert with my girlfriend, I returned to a hotel in Orlando.

This time they rolled out the red carpet. I was invited to everything.

The conference consists of two hundred troubled, angry men in windowless hotel conference rooms. They all talked about how painful and fraught sexual relations have gotten. Feminism ruined families, they said. The birth control pill ruined families. Online dating ruined families. Sex is dangerous. Touch a woman and you'll get accused of rape whenever they want.

Some were divorced men who lost custody of their children. Others were young men who were not blessed with square jawlines and broad shoulders or height, and they had failed in the headshot-based sexual marketplace of Tinder. They were obsessed with jaw exercises and tongue positioning that might help—they call it mewing, and they shared tips. (There's some truth to this: as our food has gotten softer, our jaws are indeed smaller.) They talked about body language—never lean into a girl in a photo, stand tall and strong. They were extremely deferential to more handsome muscular men, who were there mostly selling workout routines.

The men were sometimes scared of me. I was supposed to sit in a side room for a couple hours and do interviews. One buff man with a shaved head and tattoos all along his arms and up his neck sat down. But he started to shake after a minute or two and abruptly stood up and left, apologizing.

One man was onstage talking about his get-rich scheme, and he said he cured his own cancer and everyone should invest in him. I got the feeling they invited me back because they were needing liberal outrage to boost their credibility, to create some more videos about DESTROYING NYT WRITER. I took a bunch of swag—a children's book about a cruel feminist bullying a father in a supermarket, some extremely aromatic tactical soap, a hat that says Make Women Great Again—and I flew home.

I didn't have the heart to write about them in the way I knew I'd have to write about them.

A year later, the man who claimed to cure his own cancer died. I still follow some of the guys on Twitter. They're selling fitness programs and they're in-fighting again. Maybe they'll have sex with someone they pay. But a relationship is dangerous. They are Men Going Their Own Way. They won't have children. In that, they're not alone.

The night of that Los Angeles dinner party, with all the people vowing to make their lines extinct, I went home and researched sperm donors, clicking through profiles and reading through the sperm bank forums.

Alongside the women like me, I found single straight women searching. This new sperm donor customer is known as the "single mom by choice." In the forums, they explain why they're doing what they're doing. They're hoping to connect with others.

Many are facing the end of their fertile window in life. It's a sort of quiet yet frenzied scramble as their periods get a little lighter every month. They didn't want kids and then suddenly they did. Every time I've told someone that women have a biological clock, the response is invariably the same: *No no, I've got a friend who was pregnant at forty-two! No no, that's old-fashioned thinking.* It's an almost aggressive denial—like, how could you suggest the body decays? It's seen as right-wing to say that fertility ends, as though you're suggesting child brides as the alternative. And if you're rich, you absolutely can eke out a few more years with hormone shots, jamming those forty-two-year-old ovaries with as many eggs as they can fit and grow, sucking them out carefully, hoping a few are still genetically healthy. The women in the forums have had an ultrasound wand checking how many eggs are waiting half-cooked in the ovaries, and they know it's not many. Some wrote about going into debt to afford the treatments.

Mostly women in the forums barter vials of popular sold-out donors. And they suss out from existing parents if their kids with that donor turned out well, a sort of Amazon reviews for men.

One day someone strange shows up—they post that they will pay for a woman to get pregnant via sperm they buy, so long as the woman is thin and relatively healthy. A kink, I'm sure. Who knows.

Someone responds that they're interested.

Toddlers Know
Who They Are

God or Mother Earth or whoever is in charge of souls played a very strange trick on America about fifteen years ago. She put tens of thousands of souls in the wrong bodies. She put boys in girl bodies and girls in boy bodies all across the country.

It's hard to figure out whose soul is in the wrong body when a child is very little. Doctors meet babies and randomly guess their sex—"See, when you were born, you couldn't tell people who you were or how you felt. They looked at you and made a guess," reads a popular children's book about the situation. At major newspapers and in school systems, the language is that children are somewhat randomly assigned a sex at birth—"assigned female at birth," "assigned male at birth," or AFAB and AMAB for short. The true sex and gender reveals itself only with time. There is no faster way to find yourself in the middle of a struggle session than to question this. There is sometimes a special bond between a parent and a child, but on this topic there is none. Everyone in a community can be and is tasked with helping identify the child's true gender.

You can tell if a soul is in the wrong body early enough though, often when a child is a toddler. Here's the American Psychological Association defining the term: "Transgender is an umbrella term for persons whose gender identity, gender expression or behavior does not conform to that typically associated with the sex to which they were assigned at birth." You have to watch carefully for children engaging in activities *not typically associated with the sex to which they were assigned*. And these children will likely need to change genders as soon as legally possible and maybe sooner. The body must conform with the spirit. They cannot go through puberty.

If a boy-toddler is playing with dolls or wants to wear his mother's shoes, there's a good chance his soul is in the wrong body, the experts tell us.

"Young trans children know who they are," reads an *Atlantic* headline focusing on children ages three through twelve. The parenting advice website *Fatherly*: "All kids, regardless of their gender identity, start to understand their own gender typically by the age of 18 to 24 months—that's their awareness that I'm a boy, I'm a girl, I'm something totally not within that gender binary I'm seeing in the world around me. Usually, they can label that and start to share that between 18 to 24 months and up to 30 months." Signs they might be trans, from the popular publication *Insider*: "They engage in gender specific play or dress that does not correspond with the sex they were given at birth." And: "Asking questions about their own gender or LGBTQ people in general."

If a boy puts on a princess dress and likes it, that's a sign. "Alyssa tried on a pink princess dress for the first time at around age 5 and said she immediately felt 'right,'" explains *The Washington Post*, in a 2023 piece about trans identity. (Alyssa, who was born biologically male, is now in her midtwenties and quite happy as a woman, so in fact she was right.)

The mother of one trans child appeared on PBS in March 2023 to describe when she knew: "Our daughter is ten years old. She started letting us know that she was transgender really before she could even speak," says Beth, sitting next to her husband, Nathaniel.

Beth continues: "She would do things like wear her sister's clothes, pretend that towels were her long hair. And when she was about three years old she started to withdraw and become depressed, so we started doing some research."

One of our country's most prestigious hospitals for children released a series of slick, beautifully produced videos advertising their services for gender nonconforming patients.

The services include "gender affirming hysterectomies" and "chest reconstruction surgery" (formerly known as mastectomies)—all the classics of the modern pediatrician's office. The hospital put out videos with doctors saying things like, "a good portion of children do know as early as, seemingly, from the womb" and "we see a variety of young children all the way down to ages two and three." Another video says that "playing with the opposite gender toys" is an indication of transness. "Gender-affirming hysterectomy is very similar to most hysterectomies," said another doctor. The video fades to white. Then the Boston Children's Hospital logo appears.

Boston Children's Hospital has an answer to the question "When does a child know they're transgender?" Dr. Jeremi Carswell, director of the facility's Gender Multispecialty Service, sits in front of a pink background for a promotional video released by the hospital (then taken down in 2022). She's wearing a white button-down and has a sweet, calm voice.

"A child will often know that they are transgender from the moment that they have any ability to express themselves. And parents will often tell us this. We have parents who tell us that their kids, they knew from the minute they were born practically. And actions like refusing to"—the camera cuts closer—"get a haircut or standing to urinate or trying to stand to urinate"— she smiles a little—"or refusing to stand to urinate, trying on siblings' clothing, playing with quote 'opposite gender toys.'" Text comes on the screen for emphasis: *Playing with "opposite gender" toys.*

Preverbal children can send these messages all the time, says Dr. Diane Ehrensaft, who is—I'll give her whole title—a developmental and clinical psychologist, adjunct associate professor of pediatrics at the University of California, San Francisco, and director of mental health at the Child and Adolescent Gender Center, UCSF Benioff Children's Hospital.

"So the question is, what about the kids between one and two who are just developing language, or may not even have it yet? They're very action oriented. So this is where mirroring is really important and listening to actions," Dr. Ehrensaft told the audience of a conference in Santa Cruz in 2016. "So let me give you an example: I have a colleague who's transgender and there is a video of him as a toddler . . . tearing barrettes out of her hair and throwing them on the ground and sobbing. That's a gender message."

At the first signs of puberty in a gender nonconforming child who doesn't want to go through puberty, experts recommend blocking that puberty with gonadotropin-releasing hormone analogues. After that, adolescent medical transitions are sometimes warranted, though typically doctors recommend the child wait, development blocked, until their eighteenth birthday. Sometimes not. How might the puberty blocker impact brain development? If a child has been on puberty blockers since age nine, pausing development of their bodies but also maybe their brains, what does that mean? These are questions that don't have answers yet, but it's best not to think too much about that.

The clinicians for these children say it's not risky, or if it is risky, then the far greater risk is to not intervene. These children will kill themselves. They say we trust adolescents to do all kinds of things, and actually teenagers are very wise. Most of the major decisions they make are good decisions, and we just focus too much on the negative. Johanna Olson-Kennedy, the medical director for Children's Hospital Los Angeles's Center for Transyouth Health and Development, was giving a lecture one day, explaining why we should trust trans youth to decide for themselves if they are ready for surgeries, like a double mastectomy. She oversees many young people making these choices and has written a peer-reviewed paper on "chest reconstruction," or removing breasts and reforming the chest to look male.

"Actually, people get married when they're under twenty. Actually, people choose colleges to go to. Actually, people make life-altering decisions in adolescence, all the time. All the time. And honestly most of them are good," Dr. Olson-Kennedy said. "It's just the bad ones that we talk about. 'Oh my God, the cinnamon challenge!' Right? Why do we know about it? Because it's not common.

"Most teenagers aren't eating cinnamon but some are, they're on YouTube and that's stupid. But we don't put on YouTube the things that are really good decisions. Oh my gosh, my kid took the SATs. Not a very exciting after-school special. So what we do know is adolescents actually have the capacity to make a reasoned logical decision. And here's the other thing about chest surgery: if you want breasts at a later point in your life, you can go and get them."

Or as Minnesota's lieutenant governor Peggy Flanagan put it in early 2023 as she defended medical interventions for minors: "When our children tell us who they are, it is our job as grown-ups to listen and to believe them. That's what it means to be a good parent."

To go through the wrong puberty just means more surgeries

afterward. Surgeries to remove the breasts that develop, surgeries to soften the jaw that grew wide.

"For those young kids who are starting puberty and have strong gender identities that don't match their bodies, those young people can really benefit from not ever going through the wrong puberty the first time," Dr. Olson-Kennedy said. "It's much easier if we can halt their puberty early on in the process and let them be suspended for a little bit and then put them through the right puberty that corresponds to their brain."

It's hard to find good numbers on how many children have been put in the wrong bodies. But it's hundreds of thousands at least—1.4 percent of children in America between the ages of thirteen and seventeen identify as trans now, double the number from about a decade ago. The first pediatric gender clinic opened in 2007 in Boston. By 2023, there were more than sixty across the country along with countless therapists and doctors in private practice who are also seeing young patients with gender-identity issues.

If a parent resists these medical changes, they can and do lose custody of their child. Parents don't actually know their children. Who are parents to weigh in here? A child's elementary school teacher knows them much better. Doctors know them best of all. And anyway, the children know themselves. The children want to be sterilized. They do not care about bone density or breastfeeding or orgasms or any of the other things the old people go on about. It is no one's place to question them. To question the surgeries is to push your child toward suicide. Without this mastectomy, your son will kill himself. Is that what you want? The slogan is: "I'd Rather Have a Living Son Than a Dead Daughter."

<hr>

"*Childhood*. Uninterrupted." That's how the puberty-blocking implant called Supprelin is advertised. It was once given only to children suffering rare early puberties but is now quite common and popular for gender nonconforming children.

"Every single child who was truly blocked at Tanner stage 2 (9–11 years old) has never experienced orgasm," said pioneering pediatric gender surgeon Marci Bowers at a conference hosted by Duke University.

The young male who blocks his puberty very early will not be able to freeze sperm to use later because he won't have any yet. The young female won't be able to harvest eggs from ovaries that never develop. Children on puberty blockers may see their bone density crash. The enamel on their teeth may fray. The young females and young males who grow into trans men and trans women, respectively, will be able to experience love and intimacy, of course, but if they started their transition early enough, they will not orgasm.

It's inappropriate to worry about the future sex life of a child, say the experts. Why are you so focused on sex anyway? My God, why are you thinking about that child having sex? Why assume pregnancy changes anything? Devon Price, a clinical assistant professor at Loyola University Chicago's School of Continuing and Professional Studies and prominent activist on trans issues, put it this way:

"I don't know how you can believe this obsession is feminist. The obsession these people have with the bodies—and specifically the reproductive capacity—of young trans people is unsettling," Dr. Price wrote. "TERF detrans people talk a big game about how many of the people who transition will one day regret the impact it had on their fertility, and the fact they've lost 'healthy tissue' that has a 'purpose' (feeding a baby)."

To imply that a child can't make these decisions is ableist and adultist. It is to think that adults have some special power or knowledge above children.

Our body parts have no specific preordained purpose. We cannot pull out a uterus and say it is *for* anything specific. The heart is not *for* anything either. The mind is the only part of the body that matters. Our sense of self is what matters.

"And by the way, breasts aren't 'for' feeding a baby," Dr. Price wrote. "Most animals that nurse don't have breasts. . . . Your body is you, it's not an array of objects 'for' any purpose. And dividing up one's body mentally into tiny discrete parts is a huge contributor to self-objectification. It's bad for you."

No one consents to puberty anyway. No one says, yes, I'd like to go through this process today. No child is excited as their brains are wrenched from childhood and thrown into the hormonal chaos and reorganization of adolescence. Getting a first period is a shock. I didn't choose it. Puberty itself is an assault on the freedom of a child, so medication is no different.

As the trans activist Zinnia Jones wrote: "If children can't consent to puberty blockers which pause any permanent changes even with the relevant professional evaluation, how can they consent to the permanent and irreversible changes that come with their own puberty with no professional evaluation whatsoever?"

Parents in general need to be understood as oppressive.

"Parents are tyrants. 'Parent' is an oppressive class, like rich people or white people," the NBC News contributor Noah Berlatsky wrote one day. "There are things you can do to try to minimize the abuse that's endemic to the parent/child relationship, but it's always there."

The point is, these children can make decisions. They know who they are.

When I was little I played with trucks. I hated wearing dresses. I completely ignored dolls unless it was to decapitate them. This was a tomboy phase, as well-meaning adults would tell me, nodding and smiling sympathetically to my parents, who were baffled. I'd grow out of it. But when heels and makeup arrived, I hated those too. The first thing I ever bought online was a rugby ball, for some reason.

Puberty hit so hard that—God help me—I was filling out a DD cup by the eighth grade, and I hated that too. Then I realized I was attracted to other girls.

In modern parlance, I was gender nonconforming. Stage 4.

When I hear parents talk about their trans children, almost all of them describe kids *who just knew,* but then the *obviously trans* traits are just little girls vaguely drawn to boys' toys or clothes. If only my parents were more aware and more accepting, I could have been warmly counseled into pausing that unfortunate puberty. If they'd known a little better they would have offered to pay for me to be confirmed in my right gender, to get on testosterone and have my chest reconstructed nicely, flatly. I would have loved it.

There was a lot of backlash to those Boston Children's Hospital videos when they came out. People were shocked by them. There had been a series of high-profile detransitioners, the most famous of whom had started hormones or undergone surgeries as teenagers. (As an aside, there's a sense that giving a girl testosterone is less of a big deal than a mastectomy, which I think is odd.) Anyway, the detransitioners were most commonly young women, many had other mental health issues. And they felt they'd been tracked into major medical choices too fast and too young.

So it seemed alarming to then be told by so-called experts that even toddlers are actually communicating a gender message.

A few things happened during the backlash: First, the hospital took down the videos and deleted web pages about the services they offer (better to have it happen quietly). Second, the Department of Justice began threatening action against people who were seen as intimidating those doing this work.

"While free speech is indeed the cornerstone of our great nation, fear, intimidation and threats are not. I will not sit idly by," wrote then US attorney for the District of Massachusetts Rachael S. Rollins. The media careened into action to declare that the debate on whether children can consent to double mastectomies and the real videos being circulated were all just false claims. Here's NBC News at the time: "Boston Children's Hospital has warned employees about mounting threats and is coordinating with law enforcement after far-right activists on social media began targeting the hospital with false claims about its treatment of young transgender people."

It was "disinformation" to say that these surgeries happened on people under eighteen, and yet the hospital's website said it would perform vaginoplasties on children beginning at seventeen years old. (It has now disappeared from the site.) And there was this study produced by the hospital staff on the sixty-five double-mastectomy surgeries they performed on minors, the youngest being fifteen. All of this is well within the recommended practices in 2022: the World Professional Association for Transgender Health, the leading advocacy group for transgender surgeries, suggests hormones therapies can begin as young as age fourteen and surgical interventions at fifteen.

"Surgeons are focusing more attention to gender reassignment surgeries in minors," reads a 2021 literature review from the Transgender Legal Defense & Education Fund. "For the more complex surgery of vaginoplasty, over half of the surgeons practicing in this area have performed vaginoplasty on an individual under age 18. Nearly all surgeons relied on the term 'maturity' rather than chronological age to determine patients' readiness for the procedure."

You have to listen to that message. The toddler knows.

The Best Feminists
Always Have Had Balls

The best feminists of my generation were born with dicks. I don't mean it metaphorically or with any judgment because it's not a good or bad thing but an interesting one. And some of these feminists write about their dicks a lot, so I even can say with some authority that the dicks are or were good ones. Those with XY chromosomes, what we sometimes call biological males, were always a little more assertive, if you'll allow me the generalization. They are a little more comfortable with risk-taking and less averse to conflict. And so it makes sense that trans women would be the best, boldest, fiercest feminists. The only issue is that they have quite unfortunately decided that all previous generations of feminists are their first and most important enemy.

The shift from being born assigned male to becoming an adult woman might have been accompanied with surgery and hormones but not necessarily. All one needs to do to say you are a woman speaking for women is say it. The word is the act. Trans women *are women*. Or as the Human Rights Campaign puts it: "When we say women, the word includes trans women. There's no ifs, ands or buts about it. A woman's gender identity is her innermost concept of being female." Defining that feeling—what is it to feel like a woman?—then becomes the major project for this group.

The new feminists spend a lot of their writing working out what that innermost concept of *female* is. It's an old question made new. The three I'm thinking of right now:

First, there's Grace Lavery, the author of *Please Miss: A Heartbreaking Work of Staggering Penis*. She grew up in an English village, was educated at a selective boys' school, and is now an associate professor teaching Victorian literature at University of California, Berkeley, and has served as an editor of *TSQ: Transgender Studies Quarterly*.

She has blonde hair, and in photos, bright red lipstick, her expression often a little coy. She sometimes leaves a light brush of stubble visible.

Second is Andrea Long Chu, the author of *Females*, the winner of the 2023 Pulitzer Prize for Criticism. She was born in Chapel Hill, North Carolina, went to a small Christian school and then to Duke University, before getting a PhD at New York

University. Based in Brooklyn, Chu is now the book critic for *New York* magazine.

And third, less famous but influential in trans circles: Gretchen Felker-Martin, the author of *Manhunt*. She rose to prominence in the little online eddies that can buoy someone creative and smart, especially someone who also has an interest in writing dark, sexy stories. She's from rural New Hampshire, lives in a midsize city in Massachusetts, and has a Patreon to fundraise from her fans, who must be eighteen years or older to view it. She promises perks like private online movie screenings and PDFs of her novellas as they come out.

Producing smart, successful, and critically acclaimed work, these three women have taken on the project of what it means to be a female. To each of them, though in slightly different ways, to be female is to desire a certain place in society. It's an approach to life more than anything biological. As they're defining it, they're outlining a femaleness that's jarring but also very familiar. It's cozy and even comfortable for me to hear, like I've heard it before somewhere. Their conclusion is that to be a woman is, in general, disgusting.

"For our purposes, I'll define as *female* any psychic operation in which the self is sacrificed to make room for the desires of another," writes Andrea Long Chu in *Females*. "To be female is to let someone else do your desiring for you, at your own expense. This means that femaleness, while it hurts only sometimes, is always bad for you." In her telling of womanhood, femaleness is about self-negation, about letting a man desire for me, and any feelings I have contrary to that are a maleness, a masculinity of my own: "Femaleness is a universal sex defined by self-negation, against which all politics, even feminist politics, rebels. Put more simply: Everyone is female, and everyone hates it."

"The female loves herself only because she hates herself," Andrea continues. "When she makes herself beautiful—perhaps for her boyfriend or husband, perhaps for strangers on the street—she does so not out of self-regard, but because she has emptied herself out and assumed their desires as her own."

Pregnancy is a hollowing for an alien, part of a larger project of vessel-hood. "Femaleness is not an anatomical or genetic characteristic of an organism, but rather a universal existential condition."

That condition is misery: "Women hate being female as much as anybody else; but unlike everybody else, we find ourselves its select delegates."

As I read Andrea Long Chu, I was eight months pregnant with a little girl. I felt my daughter kicking and twisting.

"All efforts toward civilization are male," Chu writes. Any effort toward equal rights is an effort to stop being female, Andrea writes. Trying to get the right to vote was anti-woman. It was females trying to be men.

"Perhaps the oldest right-wing accusation brought by men and other women against feminists, whether they demanded civic equality or anti-male revolution, was that feminists were really asking, quite simply, not to be women anymore. There was a kernel of truth here," she writes. "To be for women, imagined as full human beings, is always to be against females."

That's because females are not full human beings, she explains. We are holes. Or as she puts it at another point: "distilling the femaleness to its barest essentials—an open mouth, an expectant asshole, blank, blank eyes." She draws parallels between modern women and a type of porn called *sissy porn*, in which a man is dressed like a woman and degraded for it, or put in skimpy lingerie and topped (I'm not explaining everything) by another man.

"To be a sissy is always to lose your mind. The technical term for this is *bimboification*. Captions instruct viewers to submit themselves to hypnosis, brainwashing, brain-melting, dumbing down, and other techniques for scooping out intelligence."

Sissy porn distills femaleness to its most pure form, Chu argues. Women are submissive, self-hating, lingerie-loving bottoms. We want to be penetrated and dominated, not just sexually but emotionally and—*obviously*—socially.

The people pushing back against this frame are jealous, writes Grace Lavery in *Please Miss*. Trans women are simply enjoying womanhood more. "Why are so many British people—including a sizable chunk of liberal/lefty women—hostile to trans women?" Because these old women see the narrow hips of the new feminists, the pleasure they take in female clothes and makeup, and go crazy with jealousy. Grace senses that this is what is driving the rage against her and her allies. "The problem that I refer to as *leaky boobs and the school run*, the revenge of feminist grievance against feminist pleasure, the joy of the chore; sourness as a political aesthetic; the loathing of the trans woman as a figure of pleasure embodied, of—SNIP."

The leaky boobs and the school run then become the villains of Gretchen Felker-Martin's apocalypse fantasy, *Manhunt.* There trans women are just trying to survive, and the enemies are the biological women—"the fucking chromosome crusaders." They tattoo XX on their foreheads to indicate "Pussy certified all-natural by the Daughter of the Witches You Couldn't Burn or whatever Michigan Womyn's Festival bullshit the TERFocracy in Maryland bowed down to." These women have the most annoying voices. Their voices grate.

A woman speaks, "in a voice that was cis and had always been cis and had never imagined anything but cisness, flat and opaque and interminable." In the Maryland Womyn's Legion of Felker-Martin's novel, there is of course a Captain Rodham.

It's considered in bad taste to talk about autogynephilia—or a biological male being sexually attracted to the idea of himself as a woman. It's considered a little offensive to suggest that, for some, the idea of living as a woman is a turn on. But many of the smart trans writers of the day write about it and wrestle with it quite openly. Why should it be shameful?

Chu describes the way sissy porn took over her life. Every night for a year, she slipped away from her girlfriend to secretly watch it. Often this sort of porn involves a man wearing women's clothes, makeup, and shoes and then being told how disgusting he is and how pathetic and female he is, she writes. Chu describes how it was this particular porn that got her wearing women's clothes and thinking of herself as a woman.

"About three years ago, I discovered sissy hypo videos, which in a nutshell are flashing subjective images telling you to wear panties, be girly, suck cock, and even take hormones," she writes in the book. "Nothing got me off like these. I got to the point where I started wearing panties and imagining myself as a girl when I would masturbate."

"Autogynephilia describes not an obscure paraphilia affliction but rather the basic structure of all human sexuality," she writes. "To be female is, in every case, to become what someone else wants. At bottom, everyone is a sissy. . . . At the center of sissy porn lies the asshole, a kind of universal vagina through which femaleness can always be accessed."

It can't be possible that literally everyone wants to be a woman—or else who would do all the hard work of demanding everyone wear panties?

Lavery describes the sensuality of a woman's bathroom. Why do the mommy blogs worry about this so much, she asks? "The problem is this: going to the bathroom *is* kind of sexy? At least, I have occasionally found it to be."

This all might sound fringe. A few writers. But the argument has become quite mainstream in liberal spaces. Now people are applying it to history.

If the female is submissive, an expectant hole, then how do

you explain a powerful woman? How could a Joan of Arc possibly exist and not identify as something else? Shakespeare's Globe announced they would be putting on a play about the life of Joan of Arc, and in it she is not a she at all. How could she be? Joan must have been nonbinary. She must have desired they/them pronouns. "Joan finds their power and their belief spreads like fire," the Globe announced. *The New York Times* ran an opinion piece on how the author of *Little Women*, Louisa May Alcott, ought to be considered a trans man.

Here's the paper on Louisa: "Alcott scholars agree that she felt a profound affinity with manhood. 'I am certain that Alcott never fit a binary sex-gender model,' said Gregory Eiselein, a professor at Kansas State University and the president of the Louisa May Alcott Society."

I imagine something similar being done to a historical man, like, this historical man was really submissive and quiet, so our play now reimagines him as a woman, which we think he was.

It makes sense then that something called bimbo feminism started taking off, sometimes by name but sometimes more by its ethos. Bimbo feminism is the celebration of woman as a dumb, hot object. Woman as an absolute idiot. To hell with girlbosses and equality in the boardroom. New feminism—bimboism—is about celebrating the vacant, sexual woman, the dumb woman, the hole. Being smart is capitalism.

"No more Instagrams about rising and grinding," an opinion writer at *The New York Times* told us one day in describing the trend. "No more The Wing. No more straining to be smarter than the boys. Bimboism offers an opposing and, to some, refreshing premise: Value me, look at me, not because I'm smart and diligent but for the fact that I'm not. It's anticapitalist, even antiwork."

This is a very tetchy group. Even quoting their own words will upset them. It is a group that doesn't want to be described or named. The words to depict the fleshy reality are themselves now considered off limits. But it is a very interesting group. Feminism is something that's given me a lot, so I'm invested in where it goes. The new feminists hate every wave of feminism that came before. Earth-mother fertility feminism, dyke feminism, corporate #Girlboss feminism: it's all grotesque.

Because the best feminists now know women have to go. The word *woman* fell out of fashion—too exclusionary. Pregnant people, birthing people, chest feeding, vulva-havers, period-havers: these are all normal new phrases found in public health messaging and conversation. And the little bastion of female achievement—women's sports—became the most vile holdover.

It was strange that men never experienced anything like this. *The Lancet* described women as "bodies with vaginas" but men are, well of course, men.

On the cover of the storied medical journal, it read in big letters: *Historically, the anatomy and physiology of bodies with vaginas have been neglected.*

In 2023, when Johns Hopkins University released a new glossary of terms for clinicians and others to use, they defined the lesbian as "a non-man attracted to non-men." A gay guy? "A man who is emotionally, romantically, sexually, affectionately or relationally attracted to other men."

We measure feminism in waves. The first wave was the suffragettes from the late 1800s who fought for a woman's right to be seen as an autonomous individual and to vote. By the 1960s and '70s, the second wave was about equal rights for women at work and the little things, like being able to own credit cards and decide when you have your own children. The 1990s saw a third wave focused on sexual liberation and expanding the conversation beyond wealthy white women. This wave brought feminist raunch culture and my favorite genre of music: angry young women screaming into microphones in bars across Washington State.

And now, in the 2020s, there's the fourth wave. The fourth turning. The trans revolution and the bimbo feminist.

A lot of the politics here are probably confusing to someone coming from the outside.

How do I explain that the good-liberal line now is that males have no athletic advantage over females. Or if they do, if there is even such a thing as males and females, then it's no different from some people being tall and others being short, and it's simply bigoted to separate sports by gender.

At the 2022 Sexual and Gender Minority Health Symposium, hosted by Duke University, Helen Carroll, a sports consultant for the National Center for Lesbian Rights, described trying to differentiate between male and female athletes: "If I took one hundred athletes and made a poster of them—big muscles, big hands, strong bones—you're not going to be able to tell the difference."

Or there are differences, but those just add to the normal athletic tension. Liam Miranda, a researcher at the Inclusion Playbook and former trans athlete, put it like this: "People like sports because there isn't really a level playing field." Having two different sexes competing in, let's say, rugby, certainly adds tension into the playing field.

Or from the ACLU's "debunking of myths" around trans athletes: "FACT: Trans athletes do not have an unfair advantage in sports."

It was and is considered extremely regressive to question this. When female athletes complain about the situation, about maybe not wanting to get in a boxing ring with a biological male, about feeling uncomfortable in a locker room, they're smeared as bigots.

How do I explain that it became verboten in good-liberal circles to say things like mixed-sex prison might be very dangerous to biological females, and those needs should be prioritized?

How do I explain that British feminists rallying around the statue of a suffragette were met with black bloc counterprotests? The women were going to draw attention for their cause of maintaining female-only spaces. They gathered at the statue of Emmeline Pankhurst, a British women's suffragist who died in 1928. Screaming males in balaclavas surrounded them. One of the counterprotesters: "We don't want these people coming in and standing next to this icon of feminism and the suffragette movement. They are appropriating the imagery of the suffragette movement and rebranding it as this hateful movement against trans people and we don't stand for that."

I always think about another of these protests, where one of the pro-trans protesters screamed at the biological women: "You're dinosaurs. Dinosaurs. Fossils. You're going to die out. You have failed. You have failed." They're not wrong.

As all this was happening—as I was watching progressives argue that male puberty gave no athletic advantage, that toddlers were sending gender messages, that the old feminists could die now, thanks—a rage was brewing. It was catching on with a lot of folks. A Bud Light marketing executive made a commemorative can of beer for a trans TikTok influencer with her face on it—for months the conservatives raged and boycotted. Kid Rock shot at the those darned Bud Light cans. The marketing exec lost his job, but Bud Light also lost its spot as the top-selling beer. (Modelo Especial replaced it, a better beer, so at least that part was good.) Then Target started selling dick-tucking swim trunks for penis-ed individuals who would rather have a smooth crotch, and protesters started showing up in Targets. All these things were silly in a way—beer, swimsuits. But the free-floating rage was real. For the first time, approval of same-sex marriage has been stalling and, by some polls, falling. By 2023, the backlash was here.

Part of me has felt betrayed by this: The movement wasn't focusing on basic practical issues for gays and lesbians, nor focusing on any number of countries where gay people face huge oppression or certain death. Instead the movement had gone into bizarre directions. It was obsessing on fringe cases. It was telling people that biological males who've gone through puberty have no natural advantage over women. If a movement says enough demonstrably false things to you, why believe it when it says *gay marriage is good* or *two women can raise a healthy family*?

I was feeling pretty down on all this when my wonderful synagogue announced that the toddler service next week—the Tot Shabbat, it's called—would be a drag show. I was feeling, honestly, a little crazed about it all—*these doctors are neutering little gay kids* was my tone at dinner parties. *Everyone is erasing women* was something I would try to bring up in really inappropriate settings.

The organizations that got me my white-picket-fence life that I love and the safety to raise a family were run by people arguing children can consent to cross-sex hormones. For a straight person, this can all be an oddity. For a gay person, this is a crisis. But the radicalism of the movement was hardening me.

And now here was our great synagogue, and the toddlers, and the upcoming drag queen.

Drag Queen Story Hour had become an increasingly politicized obsession throughout 2023, with some on the right protesting outside public libraries that were hosting one for the kids, and progressives deciding in turn that all events in fact needed drag queens, like they were a priestly caste to bless every story hour and baseball game. Every Tot Shabbat.

The next week we showed up to the synagogue as usual. A drag queen came out. I'll admit right off the bat she looked fabulous. Our daughter's main agenda in Tot Shabbat is chewing on chairs. In her defense the Tot Shabbat was sometimes a little light on Jewish content (a lot of "Wheels on the Bus"). But she paused her gnawing to admire the wig, the dress, the heels.

Then the strangest thing happened: The drag queen proceeded to give a very, *very* deeply Jewish Tot Shabbat. There was no "Wheels on the Bus." She put on a prayer shawl and sang traditional Jewish songs for half an hour. Her outfit mesmerized our daughter the whole time.

Watching her I remembered being at drag bars as a teenager and how amazingly fun it was, how relaxed a drag queen can make everyone. I softened. It's a very old art, men dressing as exaggerated women for laughs. Afterward Miss Livinya sat for photos and toddlers sat on her lap like she was Santa. Our daughter loved it and so did I. The best Tot Shabbat drag queens have . . .

Part IV

MORNING AFTER

The Failure
of San Francisco

San Francisco was conquered by the United States in 1846, and two years later, the new Americans discovered gold. That's about when my ancestors came—my German great-great-great-grandfather worked at a butcher shop on Jackson Street before starting what would become a massive cattle ranch. The gold dried up but too many young men with outlandish dreams remained. The little city, prone to earthquakes and fires, kept growing. The Beats came, then the hippies; the moxie and hubris of the place remained.

My grandmother's favorite insult was to call someone dull. I learned young that it was impolite to point when a naked man passed by, groceries in hand. If someone wanted to travel by unicycle or be a white person with dreadlocks or raise a child communally among a group of gays or live on a boat or start a ridiculous-sounding company, that was just fine. Behind the bead curtains of my aunt's house, I learned you had to let your strangeness breathe.

It was always weird, always a bit dangerous. Once, when I was very little, a homeless man grabbed me by the hair, lifting me into the air for a moment before the guy dropped me as my dad yelled. For years I told anyone who would listen that I'd been kidnapped. But every compromise San Francisco demanded was worth it. The hills are so steep that I didn't learn to ride a bike until high school, but every day I saw the bay, and the cool fog rolling in over the water. When puberty hit, I asked the bus driver to drop me off where the lesbians were, and he did. A passenger shouted that he hoped I'd find a nice girlfriend, and I waved back, smiling, my mouth full of braces and rubber bands.

So much has been written about the beauty and mythology of this city that it's superfluous to add even a little more to the ledger. If he ever got to heaven, Herb Caen, the town's beloved old chronicler, once said he'd look around and say, "It ain't bad, but it ain't San Francisco." The cliffs, the stairs, the cold clean air, the low-slung beauty of the Sunset District, the cafés tucked along narrow streets, then Golden Gate Park drawing you down from the middle of the city all the way to the beach. It's so goddamn whimsical and inspiring and temperate; so full of redwoods and wild parrots and the smell of weed and sourdough, brightly painted homes and backyard chickens, lines for the oyster bar and gorgeous men in chaps at the leather festival. The beauty and the mythology—the preciousness, the self-regard—are part of what has almost killed it. And I, now in early middle age, sometimes wish it weren't so nice at all.

I do need you to love San Francisco a little bit, like I do a lot, in order to hear the story of how my city nearly fell apart. Because San Francisco was where every progressive idea bumping around America came to be tried out.

On a cold, sunny day not too long ago, I went to see the city's new Tenderloin Center for drug addicts on Market Street. It was downtown, an open-air chain-link enclosure in what used to be a public plaza. On the sidewalks all around it, people were lying on the ground, twitching. There was a free mobile shower, laundry, and bathroom station emblazoned with the words DIGNITY ON WHEELS. A young man was lying next to it, stoned, his shirt riding up, his face puffy and sunburned. Inside the enclosure, services were doled out: food, medical care, clean syringes, referrals for housing. It was basically a safe space to shoot up. The city government said it was trying to help. But from the outside, what it looked like was young people being eased into death on the sidewalk, surrounded by half-eaten boxed lunches.

By chance, when I arrived at the safe-use enclosure in that public square, they were kicking out a friend of mine. He's an activist-journalist type who was trying to see what was going on. The city very much did not want anyone doing this. When I tried to talk to the people manning the gate, pudgy city workers with name tags told me I wasn't welcome there, nor would they answer basic questions about what goes on there. Someone started video recording me and another person started peppering me with questions—who was I, where was I from? What happened in that public square, now cordoned off with a privacy fence, was secret. Inside was something intimate, almost sacred. City workers and the activists around them agreed that helping someone get sober isn't the goal anymore. Only the city workers know how to properly guide this community into their peaceful death, and it would be much better if I stopped asking questions and let them do what they do best. It's an intimate, private moment—on public ground—between the city and the addict.

Months later, as pressure mounted, the Tenderloin Center welcomed a small tour of reporters to walk through, but then the drug arena was shut down.

A couple of years ago, this was an intersection full of tourists and office workers who coexisted, somehow, with the large and ever-present community of the homeless. I've walked the corner a thousand times. Now the homeless—and those who care for the homeless—are the only ones left.

During the first year or so of the pandemic, San Francisco County lost more than one in twenty residents. (I was among the departures.) Signs of the city's pandemic decline were everywhere—the boarded-up stores, the ghostly downtown, the encampments. But walking these streets awakened me to how bad San Francisco had gotten even before the coronavirus hit—to how much suffering and squalor I'd come to think was normal.

Stepping over people's bodies, blurring my eyes to not see a dull needle jabbing and jabbing again between toes—it coarsened me. I'd gotten used to the idea that some people just want to live like that. I was even a little defensive of it: *Hey, it's America. It's your choice.*

If these ideas seem facile or perverse, well, they're not the only ones I'd come to have. Before I left, I'd gotten used to the idea of housing so expensive that it would, as if by some natural law, force couples out of town as soon as they had a kid. According to US Census data from 2020, San Francisco now has the fewest children per capita of any large American city, and according to California's Department of Housing, in 2023 an annual salary of $149,000 counts as low income for a family of four.

I'd gotten used to the crime, rarely violent but often brazen; to leaving the car empty and the doors unlocked so thieves would at least quit breaking my windows. A lot of people leave notes on the glass stating some variation of *Nothing's in the car. Don't smash the windows.* One time someone smashed our windows just to steal a scarf. Once, when I was walking and a guy tore my jacket off my back and sprinted away with it, I didn't even shout for help. I was embarrassed—what was I, *a tourist?* Living in a failing city does weird things to you. The normal thing to do then was to yell, to try to get help—even, dare I say it, from a police officer—but this felt somehow weak and maybe racist.

A couple of years ago, one of my friends saw a man staggering down the street, bleeding. She recognized him as someone who regularly slept outside in the neighborhood, and called 911. Paramedics and police arrived and began treating him, but members of a homeless advocacy group noticed and intervened. They told the man that he didn't have to get into the ambulance, that he had the right to refuse treatment. So that's what he did. The paramedics left; the activists left. The man sat on the sidewalk alone, still bleeding. A few months later, he died about a block away.

It was easier to ignore this kind of suffering amid the throngs of workers and tourists. And you could always avert your gaze and look at the beautiful city around you. But in lockdown the beauty became obscene. The city couldn't get kids back into the classroom; many people were living on the streets; petty crime was rampant. I used to tell myself that San Francisco's politics were wacky but the city was trying—really trying—to be good. But the reality is that with the smartest minds and so much money and the very best of intentions, San Francisco became a cruel city. It became so dogmatically progressive that maintaining the purity of the politics required accepting—or at least ignoring—devastating results.

If you're going to die on the street, San Francisco is not a bad place to do it. The fog keeps things temperate. There's nowhere in the world with more beautiful views. City workers and volunteers bring you food and blankets, needles and tents. Doctors come to see how the fentanyl is progressing, and to make sure the rest of you is alright as you go.

In February 2021, at a corner in the lovely Japantown neighborhood, just a few feet from a house that would soon sell for

$4.8 million, a thirty-seven-year-old homeless man named Dustin Walker died by the side of the road. His body lay there for at least eleven hours. He wore blue shorts and even in death clutched his backpack.

I can't stop thinking about how long he lay there, dead, on that corner, and how normal this was in our putatively gentle city. San Franciscans are careful to use language that centers people's humanity—you don't say "a homeless person"; you say "someone experiencing homelessness"—and yet we live in a city where many of those people die on the sidewalk.

The budget to tackle homelessness and provide supportive housing has been growing exponentially for years. In 2021, the city announced that it would pour more than $1 billion into the issue over the next two years. In 2019, the city's homeless census counted 8,000 people in one day; three years later, all these efforts had reduced the number of homeless to 7,754.

Alison Hawkes, a spokesperson for the Department of Public Health, said money spent on the well-being of the homeless goes to good use: many people "end up remaining on the street but in a better situation. Their immediate needs are taken care of."

You can't blame the plague of meth and opioids on my hometown. Fentanyl is a national catastrophe. But people addicted to drugs come from all over the country in part for the services San Francisco provides. In addition to the supervised drug-use facility in the plaza, San Francisco had a specially sanctioned and city-maintained slum a block from city hall, where food, medical care, and counseling are free, and every tent costs taxpayers roughly $60,000 a year. People addicted to fentanyl come, too, because buying and doing drugs here is so easy. In 2014, Proposition 47, a state law, downgraded drug possession from a felony to a misdemeanor—one that wouldn't get prosecuted.

This approach to drug use and homelessness is distinctly San Franciscan, blending empathy-driven progressivism with California libertarianism. The city has always had a soft spot for vagabonds, and an admirable focus on care over punishment. Policymakers and residents largely embraced the exciting idea that people should be able to do whatever they want to do, including live in tent cities and have fun with drugs and make their own medical decisions, even if they are out of their minds sometimes. But then fentanyl arrived, and more and more people started dying in those tents. When the pandemic began, the drug crisis got worse.

San Francisco saw ninety-two drug deaths in 2015. There were about seven hundred in 2020. By way of comparison, that year, 261 San Franciscans died of Covid. And the new level of death shows no sign of slowing. By 2023, there were more than seven hundred drug overdose deaths.

In 2019, someone posted a picture in a Facebook group called B.A.R.T. Rants & Raves, where people complain about the state of the regional transportation system. The photo was of a young man, slumped over on a train. People were chiming in about how gross the city was.

A woman named Jacqui Berlinn wrote in the comments, simply: "That's my son."

His name is Corey Sylvester and he was thirty-one years old.

She posted a photo of him when he was sober: "May he return there soon."

Berlinn has five children, and is also raising Sylvester's daughter. Since she posted that comment, she's become an activist, calling on the city to crack down on drug sales, put dealers in jail, and arrest her son so that he's forced to become sober in jail, which she sees as the only way to save his life. She told me that she feels San Francisco has failed people like him: "Nothing that is being done is improving the situation."

We met on a stoop by the Civic Center, where her son used to hang out. She hadn't seen him in months, but she spoke with him periodically. She cried as she talked about his journey into drugs. She said he was a heroin addict. He'd get sober after stints in jail, but it wouldn't last. "I'd see him sometimes, and he didn't look that bad, and that was how it was for ten years," she told me. "But then the dealers started putting fentanyl in everything, and being on fentanyl, it's changed him, deteriorated him so rapidly . . . Before, he looked pretty healthy and smiling. And now he's got this stoop. He walks almost at a forty-degree angle, like an old man."

He'd been stabbed twice. He got an infection in his thumb, and she thought he might lose the hand. "They need to stop ignoring the fact that there are people out here selling fentanyl on the streets," she said. "When it was just heroin—I can't believe I'm saying 'just heroin.' Fentanyl is different. We're normalizing people dying."

One day, Berlinn was out looking for Corey in the Tenderloin neighborhood when she came across someone else's son. "He was naked in front of Safeway ... And he was saying he was God and he was eating a cardboard box."

She called the police. Officers arrived but said there was nothing they could do; he said he didn't want help, and he wasn't hurting anyone. "They said it's not illegal to be naked; people are in the Castro naked all the time ... They just left him naked eating cardboard on the street in front of Safeway."

What happened to the man at the Safeway, what happened to Dustin Walker—these are parables of a sort of progressive-libertarian nihilism, of the belief that any intervention that has to be imposed on a vulnerable person is so fundamentally flawed and problematic that the best thing to do is nothing at all. Anyone offended by the sight of the suffering is just judging someone who's having a mental-health episode. Any liberal who argues that the state can and should take control of someone in the throes of drugs and psychosis is basically a Republican. If and when the vulnerable person dies, that was his choice, and in San Francisco we congratulate ourselves on being very accepting of that choice.

In 2021, a few blocks from my childhood home, I bought my wife her wedding ring at a beautiful little antique store. It was ransacked a few months later. The shaken owner posted a video; the showcases were empty and the whole place was covered in glass.

You can spend days debating San Francisco crime statistics and their meaning, and many people do. It has relatively low rates of violent crime, and when compared with similarly sized cities, one of the lowest rates of homicide. But what the city has become notorious for are crimes like shoplifting and car break-ins, and there the data show that the reputation is earned. Burglaries are up more than 40 percent since 2019. Car break-ins have declined lately, but San Francisco still suffers more car break-ins—and far more property theft overall—per capita than cities like Los Angeles and Atlanta.

The head of CVS Health's organized-crime division has called San Francisco "one of the epicenters of organized retail crime." Thefts in San Francisco's Walgreens stores are four times the national average. Stores are reducing hours or shutting down. Seven Walgreens locations closed over a period of four months, and some point to theft as the reason. The city's response was to brush it off, saying that the stores were just closing low-revenue locations. And while about 70 percent of shoplifting cases in San Francisco ended in an arrest in 2011, by 2021, only 15 percent did.

The movement to decriminalize shoplifting in San Francisco began in 2014 with Proposition 47, the state law that downgraded drug possession and also recategorized the theft of merchandise worth less than $950 as a misdemeanor. It accelerated in 2019 with the election of Chesa Boudin as district attorney.

The election of Boudin was thrilling for the city. It occurred during the heights of rage against President Donald Trump, when more and more white people were becoming aware of police violence against black people and demanding criminal justice reforms. London Breed, the city's first black female mayor, wanted a liberal moderate for district attorney, but Boudin ran to the left as a fierce progressive ideologue whose worldview was shaped by his imprisoned parents, members of the Weather Underground. He was a public defender, not a prosecutor at all. He had worked in Venezuela and in 2009 congratulated the former dictator Hugo Chávez for abolishing term limits. Boudin was a charismatic figure. His campaign manager called him "a national movement candidate."

The Police Officers Association fought hard against him, spending $400,000 on a barrage of attack ads, according to the *San Francisco Examiner*. They didn't work. At Boudin's election party, a city supervisor led the crowd in a chant of "Fuck the POA." During his campaign, Boudin said he wouldn't prosecute quality-of-life crimes. He wanted to "break the cycle of recidivism" by addressing the social causes of crime—poverty, addiction, mental-health issues. Boudin was selling revolution, and San Francisco was ready. In theory.

But not in fact. Because it turns out that people on the Left also own property, and generally believe stores should be allowed to have intact windows and be paid for the goods they sell.

It had become no big deal to see someone stealing in San Francisco. Videos of crimes in progress go nationally viral fairly often. One from 2021 shows a group of people fleeing a Neiman Marcus with goods in broad daylight. Others show people grabbing what they can from drugstores and walking out. There's no chase. The cashiers are blasé about it at this point. Aisle after aisle of deodorant and shampoo are under lock and key. Press a button for the attendant to get your dish soap.

But the San Francisco experiment, as pioneered under Boudin, was to do very little prosecution of crimes. Under Boudin, prosecutors in the city could no longer use the fact that someone has been convicted of a crime in the past to ask for a longer sentence, except in "extraordinary circumstances." Boudin ended cash bail and limited the use of "gang enhancements" on sentences, which allow harsher sentences for gang-related felonies. In most cases he prohibited prosecutors from seeking charges when drugs and guns were found during minor traffic stops. "We will not charge cases determined to be a racist pretextual stop that leads to recovery of contraband," Rachel Marshall, the district attorney's director of communications, told me.

Marshall is one of Boudin's on-staff Twitter soldiers. She was combative as I tried to gather facts about what really happened in San Francisco, even denying things her office had previously been proud to say they did. It became a bit surreal.

Boudin announced on July 9, 2021: "This week, we launched a project to expunge nonviolent, low-level convictions for 37,000+ eligible SF residents."

A fact-checker wrote to Marshall, asking simply, "Is it accurate to say that, as district attorney, Chesa Boudin launched a project to expunge 37,000 low-level convictions?"

"No," Marshall responded.

Boudin is a big proponent of "collaborative courts" that focus on rehabilitation over jail time, such as Veterans Justice Court and Behavioral Health Court. Under his tenure they began to try more cases than ever before. In 2018, less than 40 percent of petty-theft cases were sent to these programs, compared with more than 70 percent in 2021. Marshall said it's the judges who decide which cases to divert, not Boudin, and eligibility rules for the collaborative courts have loosened in recent years. But critics also pointed out that Boudin is getting fewer convictions overall: 40 percent in 2021, compared with about 60 percent under his predecessor.

About sixty prosecutors have left since Boudin took office—close to half of his team. Some retired or were fired, but others quit in protest. I talked with two who have since joined a campaign to recall him. One of them, a homicide prosecutor named Brooke Jenkins, told me she left in part because Boudin was pressuring some lawyers to prosecute major crimes as lesser offenses. (Marshall said this was "a lie.") She couldn't be part of it. "The victims feel hopeless," Jenkins told me. "They feel he has lost their opportunity for justice. Right now what they see and feel is that his only concern is the criminal offender."

A 2020 tweet from the Tenderloin police station captures the frustration of the rank and file: "Tonight, for the fifteenth (15th) time in 18 months, and the 3rd time in 20 days, we are booking the same suspect at county jail for felony motor vehicle theft."

Boudin has a rugged jawline and fast, tight answers for his critics. His office vehemently rejected the argument that he's not doing enough to tackle crime. "The DA has filed charges in about 80 percent of felony drug sales and possession for sales cases presented to our office by police," Marshall pointed out. After all, he can prosecute people only if the police arrest them, and arrest rates have plummeted under his tenure. So how can that be his fault? But *why* have arrest rates plummeted? The pandemic is one reason. Perhaps it's also because the DA said from the beginning that he would not prioritize the prosecution of lower-level offenses. Police officers generally don't arrest people they know the DA won't charge.

In 2020, I interviewed Boudin while working on a story. When we talked about why he wasn't interested in prosecuting quality-of-life crimes, he explained that street crime is small potatoes compared with the high-level stuff he wants to focus on. ("Kilos, not crumbs" is a favorite line.) He has suggested that many drug dealers in San Francisco are themselves vulnerable and in need of protection. "A significant percentage of people selling drugs in San Francisco—perhaps as many as half—are here from Honduras," he said in a 2020 virtual town hall. "We need to be mindful about the impact our interventions have. Some of these young men have been trafficked here under pain of death. Some of them have had family members in Honduras who have been or will be harmed if they don't continue to pay off the traffickers."

A lot of this does make sense. It's not right to incarcerate people accused but not convicted of crimes for unfair lengths of time. No one wants immigrants' relatives to be killed by MS-13. Few of Boudin's policy ideas—individually, and sometimes with reasonable limitations—are indefensible. (Ending cash bail for truly minor offenses, for instance, protects people from losing their job or their home while in jail.) But, as with homelessness, the city's overall take on criminal justice reform moved well past the point of common sense. In spring of 2022, a man who had been convicted of fifteen burglary and theft-related felonies from 2002 to 2019 was rearrested on sixteen new counts of burglary and theft. Most of those charges were dismissed and he was released on probation. It really didn't inspire confidence that the city was taking any of this seriously.

Boudin's defenders liked to dismiss his critics as whiny tech bros or rich right-wingers. One pro-Boudin flyer said *Stop the right-wing agenda*. But the drumbeat of complaints came from plenty of good liberals, and, when the recall came, that's also who voted against him. If it were only the rich, well, the rich can hire private security, or move to the suburbs. And many do. They're not the only people who live here, and they're not the only ones who got angry.

Nothing did more to alienate San Francisco's liberal home-owning middle class over the years than how the progressive leaders managed the city's housing crisis.

Consider the story of the flower farm at 770 Woolsey Street. It slopes down 2.2 acres in the sunny southern end of the city and is filled with run-down greenhouses, the glass long shattered—a chaos of birds and wild roses. For five years, advocates fought a developer who was trying to put sixty-three units on that bucolic space. They wanted to sell flowers there and grow vegetables for the neighborhood—a kind of banjo-and-beehives fantasy. The thing they didn't want—at least not there, not on that pretty hill—was a big housing development. Who wants to argue against them? In San Francisco the word *developer* is basically a slur, something worse than calling someone a Republican. What kind of monster wants to bulldoze wild roses?

Decades of progressive governance in San Francisco yielded a thicket of regulations—safety reviews, environmental reviews, historical reviews, sunlight-obstruction reviews—that empower residents to essentially paralyze development. It costs only $682 to file for a discretionary review that can hold up a construction project for years—if you're an established club that's been around for at least two years, it's free. Plans for one nineteen-unit development geared toward the middle class were halted in 2022 because, among other issues raised by the neighbors, the building would have increased overall shadow coverage on Dolores Park by 0.001 percent.

The cost of real estate hit crisis levels in the 2010s, as ambitious grads from all over the world crammed into the hills to work in the booming tech industry. Soon, there was nowhere for them to live. Tech workers moved into RVs, parked alongside the poor and unhoused. Illegal dorms sprang up. Well-paid young people gentrified almost every neighborhood in town. In 2018, when London Breed was elected mayor at the age of forty-three, she had only just stopped living with a roommate; she couldn't afford to live alone.

Existing homeowners, meanwhile, got very, very rich. If all other tactics fail, neighbors who oppose a big construction project can just put it on the ballot. If given a choice, who would ever vote to risk their property value going down, or say, "Yes, I'm fine with a shadow over my backyard"? It doesn't happen.

Rage against this pleasant status quo has come from a faction of young renters. I once went to a training session in the Mission District run by a pro-housing group called YIMBY—for "Yes in My Backyard." I watched a PowerPoint presentation—"And here's another reason to be mad at your grandparents! Next slide"—and then joined the group for drinks.

"The elderly NIMBYs literally hiss at people," said Steven Buss, who now runs a moderate organizing team called GrowSF, about the tension during community housing meetings. (One foggy night, at one of those meetings, I heard the hissing, and it was funny, and the project they were talking about never got built.)

Gabe, a lawyer, popped in: "I love kale too, but you could house fifty kids and their families on that site. It's about priorities. They want a farm. A farm does not serve the common good. I can't tell them not to want it—but I can tell them that housing is what we need more. I don't want to end up surrounded by a bunch of super-rich people and a farm."

The city's progressives seem to feel that San Francisco is just too beautiful and fragile to change. The city is complete. Any change will mean diminishment; any new, bigger building means the old, charming one is gone, and the old, charming resident is probably gone too. The flow of newcomers is out of control; they should just stop coming here. The community gardens have to stay, along with the sunlight spilling across the low buildings. No one thinks about it as damning teachers and firefighters to mega-commutes. No one thinks of it as kicking out the middle class. Given the choice between housing people in sidewalk tents or in new buildings that might risk blocking an inch of their view of the bay, San Franciscans, for years, chose the tents.

The anger directed at Chesa Boudin probably could have been contained. The homeless and the street drugs were bad, but it was, at least, fairly consolidated. The petty crime was frustrating, but it wasn't what lit the city up for revolution. The housing crush was miserable, but it's been that way for more than a decade now.

The spark that lit this all on fire was the school board. The population most ready to rage was San Francisco's parents.

The city's schools were shut for most of the 2020–21 academic year—longer than schools in most other cities, and much longer than San Francisco's private schools. In the middle of the pandemic, with no real reopening plan in sight, school board meetings became major events, with audiences on Zoom of more than one thousand. The board didn't have unilateral power to reopen schools even if it wanted to—that depended on negotiations between the district, the city, and the teachers' union—but many parents were appalled to find that the board members didn't even seem to want to talk much about getting kids back into classrooms. They didn't want to talk about learning loss or issues with attendance and functionality. It seemed they couldn't be bothered with topics like ventilation. Instead they wanted to talk about white supremacy.

One night in 2021, a school board meeting lasted seven hours, one of which was devoted to making sure a man named Seth Brenzel stayed off the parent committee.

Brenzel is a music teacher, and at the time he and his husband had a child in public school. Eight seats on the committee were open, and Brenzel was unanimously recommended by the other committee members. But there was a problem: Brenzel is white.

"My name's Mari," one attendee said. "I'm an openly queer parent of color that uses *they/them* pronouns." They noted that the parent committee was already too white—out of ten sitting members, three were white. This was "really, really problematic," board members said. "I bet there are parents that we can find that are of color and that also are queer . . . QTPOC voices need to be led first before white queer voices."

Someone else called in, identifying herself as Cindy. She was calling to defend Brenzel, and she was crying. "He is a gay father of a mixed-race family," she said.

A woman named Brandee came on the call: "I'm a white parent and have some intersectionality within my family. My son has several disabilities. And I really wouldn't dream of putting my name forward for this." She had some choice words for Cindy: "When white people share these kinds of tears at board meetings"—she paused, laughing—"I have an excellent book suggestion for you. It's called *White Tears/Brown Scars*. I'd encourage you to read it, thank you."

Alison Collins, a member of the school board, dealt the death blow: "As a mixed-race person myself, I find it really offensive when folks say that somebody's a parent of somebody who's a person of color, as, like, a signifier that they're qualified to represent that community."

Brenzel remained mostly expressionless throughout the meeting. He did not speak. Eventually the board agreed to defer the vote. He was never approved.

The other big debate on these Zoom calls was whether to rechristen schools named for figures such as Abraham Lincoln, Paul Revere, and Dianne Feinstein, the first female mayor of San Francisco. The board labeled these figures symbols of a racist past, and ultimately voted to rename forty-four "injustice-linked" schools.

Their conviction did not persist. After a backlash and nationwide mockery, the board suspended the implementation of the changes.

The board members were just doing what they had been put there to do. Collins and her two most progressive colleagues were elected in 2018, the year before Boudin, in a rush of enthusiasm. Collins had a blog focused on justice in education, and there was a sense that she would champion a radical new politics. But during the endless lockdown, enthusiasm began to wane, even among many people who'd voted for her. They found themselves turned off by the board's combative tone. It turned out they also didn't like the board's actual ideas about education.

In February 2021, board members agreed that they would avoid the phrase *learning loss* to describe what was happening to kids locked out of their classrooms. Instead they would use the words *learning change*. Schools being shut just meant students were "having different learning experiences than the ones we currently measure," Gabriela López, a member of the board at the time, said. "They are learning more about their families and their cultures." Framing this as some kind of "deficit" was wrong, the board argued.

That same month, the board voted to replace the rigorous test that screened applicants for Lowell, San Francisco's most competitive high school, with a lottery system. López had explained it this way: "Grades and standardized test scores are automatic barriers for students outside of white and Asian communities." She said they "have shown to be one of the most effective racist policies, considering they're used to attempt to measure aptitude and intelligence. So the fact that Lowell uses this merit-based system as a step in applying is inherently racist."

Collins echoed that: "'Merit' is an inherently racist construct designed and centered on white supremacist framing."

If you didn't like these changes, tough. A parent on Twitter accused López of trying to destroy the school system, and she replied with the words, "I mean this sincerely" followed by a middle-finger emoji. In July, on the topic of people saying they'd leave town due to the declining quality of life in San Francisco, López wrote, "I'm like, then leave."

Gabriela López must have thought that history was on her side. Boudin too. But things are turning out differently. If there was a tipping point in this story, it was when the city's Asian American parents in particular got really, really mad.

Alison Collins's profile rose as well during the pandemic. She was particularly famous for the renaming-schools debacle, and also for refusing to hire consultants to study the impact of not reopening schools. People started looking through her old tweets. In 2016, she had written: "Many Asian Americans believe they benefit from the 'model minority' BS. In fact many Asian American teachers, students and parents actively promote these myths. They use white supremacist thinking to assimilate and 'get ahead.'"

Collins, who is black, also complained about Asian Americans not speaking out enough about Trump: "Do they think they won't be deported? Profiled? Beaten? Being a house n****r is still being a n****r. You're still considered 'the help.'"

About a third of the San Francisco population is Asian.

"Her comments deeply insulted my family and the entire Chinese community in San Francisco," Kit Lam told me. Lam is an immigrant from Hong Kong with two children in public school. He worked for the school district, in the enrollment department, though when we spoke he had just learned that his job was being eliminated. He said he knew what richer parents were doing during the pandemic because he saw the paperwork: they were pulling their kids out and sending them to private schools. Lam didn't have that choice.

In April 2021, he started going on 1400 AM, the Bay Area's Chinese-language radio station, to express his outrage. He spoke out against school closures and the decision to get rid of the admissions test for Lowell. Asian students have traditionally been overrepresented at Lowell; getting in is one of the best ways for high-achieving poor and middle-class kids in San Francisco to rise up the economic ladder.

This was how he became a community organizer. He and others began gathering signatures and raising money for a campaign to recall Collins, López, and another progressive board member, Faauuga Moliga. Siva Raj, another of the recall organizers, told me that roughly half of those volunteering for the campaign spoke Chinese.

A member of the board asked Collins to voluntarily step down. She refused. Instead, she sued five of her fellow members. She also sued the district. She asked for $87 million, citing, among other afflictions, "severe mental and emotional distress," "damage to self-image," and "injury to spiritual solace."

Her case was tossed. And in February 2022, San Franciscans voted decisively to remove all three from the board. A landslide 76 percent voted to recall Collins; the other two were recalled by about 70 percent each. They have been replaced by moderates, appointed by the mayor. Collins and López slammed their opponents as agents of white supremacy, but the turnout was diverse, and impressive, especially for a special election: more people actually voted to recall the board members than had cast votes for them in the first place.

My hometown isn't turning red on any electoral maps. But the shift is real. The farm at 770 Woolsey? The developer finally has approval to turn it into housing.

Just a few months after the school board recall, Chesa Boudin faced his own recall election. Boudin's opponents, likewise, came from all over the city. He said they were funded by elites—and venture capitalists, private school supporters, and a Republican hedge fund manager did fund a lot of it. Plus, the recall campaign did raise about twice as much money as the campaign to support him. But wealthy people had donated to the pro-Boudin campaign too. The racial group that was *most likely to say* they wanted Boudin recalled? Asian Americans. Their allies included many from the remnants of the city's middle class, as well as the same sort of swayable liberals who went from voting for Collins to recalling her.

In June, Boudin was recalled. Brooke Jenkins ran to serve out the rest of his term and won.

Just a few years ago, London Breed had proudly embraced the "defund the police" movement; no longer. In spring of 2022, after the city's gay-pride parade banned police officers from marching in uniform, Breed announced that, in solidarity, she wouldn't march either.

I took a stroll with her one day. She had just given a press conference on anti-Asian hate crimes outside a senior center in Chinatown. Like other cities during the pandemic, San Francisco had seen a spike in the reporting of hate crimes against Asians. People were scared. Breed grew up in the city's projects and knows residents who have had family members shot and killed recently.

"I know a lot of people who supported Chesa because there was a strong push for criminal justice," she told me. "I don't think people believed that it meant that justice would not occur."

"That's not justice reform, if everyone who commits the crime is getting off for the crime," she said.

As we talked, we walked through Chinatown, then up past the $7 million homes of Russian Hill and down into North Beach. The bay lay ahead; the cable-car drivers waved to the mayor; the city's problems seemed far off. But Breed was angry, disappointed with the progressive faction and how it had let the city down. A few months earlier, Breed had announced a new approach to crime, starting with the Tenderloin, whose streets and sidewalks are full of fentanyl's chaos. She declared it to be in a state of emergency and approved three months of funding for increased law enforcement there.

The order was mostly symbolic. The drug problem isn't limited to a few bad blocks. Often a sweep of the homeless just means pushing the tents and dealers down the road. And anyone who lives in San Francisco knows the Tenderloin has been an emergency for years. But it enabled the mayor to trot out some new rhetoric: "What I'm proposing today and what I will be proposing in the future will make a lot of people uncomfortable, and I don't care." It was time, she said, to be "less tolerant of all the bullshit that has destroyed our city."

Eventually, people want the man who killed the dog to be arrested. Eventually, the streets are so full of tents you can't see a sidewalk and your favorite camera shop is broken into so many times it closes, and you think: *There's got to be a better way here.* People can be bullied or gaslit into ignoring all kinds of things for a while, but eventually, people's willingness to put up with the bad stuff cracks. Dogmatism buckles under pressure from reality. According to city data, in 2023 San Francisco recorded 806 overdose deaths, a grim new record. It's hard to argue that the solution is just to do the same things as before but more.

Voters threw out half the school board too. It was a landslide. They did it because none of those characters seemed to care that they were making the citizens of our city miserable in service of an ideology that made sense everywhere but in reality. There is a sense that, on everything from housing to schools, San Francisco had lost the plot—that the progressive leaders here have been LARPing left-wing values instead of working to create an actual livable city. And many San Franciscans had had enough.

Residents had hoped Boudin would reform the criminal justice system and treat low-level offenders more humanely. Instead, his policies victimized victims, allowed criminals to go free to reoffend, and did nothing to help the city's most vulnerable. The fight was leftists versus liberals. It was between idealists who think a perfect world is within reach—it'll only take a little more time, a little more commitment, a little more funding, forever—and those who are fed up.

If progressives have overplayed their hand, gotten a little decadent in culture-war wins and stirring slogans, without the good government to back them all up, San Francisco is showing the way toward an internal reformation.

Before the school board vote, the last local recall in San Francisco was in 1983. There has not been this level of conflict at farmers' markets, where dueling signature-gatherers face off across from the organic-dog-treat kiosk, in almost forty years. This is, in part, because until recently many San Franciscans were afraid. If a tech worker complained, they were *reviled*. If an aging hippie complained, they were a racist old nut. It was easier to blame all of our issues on outsiders—those Silicon Valley interlopers who came in and ruined the city. The drugs, the homelessness, the crime—blame the Google employees who skewed the city's condo market and brought in their artisanal chocolates, their scooters, their trendy barbers. If not for them and the inequality they created, San Francisco would still be good.

There's some truth to that: you cannot tell the story of the housing crunch without the tech boom. But people started looking at city hall, and at the school board. They realized there were no tech bros there. The fentanyl epidemic and the pandemic cracked something. With the city locked down endlessly, with people dying in the streets, with schools closed, it was slowly becoming OK to say *Maybe this is ridiculous. Maybe this isn't working.*

Of course, it'll take more than a couple of recall votes to save San Francisco. When I asked Breed about the new center for addicts in the plaza—the creation of which she supported—she seemed a little uncomfortable and soon after wanted to wrap up our interview. She said something vague about how not all change can happen at once.

NIMBYism and fentanyl are as much a part of the San Francisco landscape now as the bridge and the fog. And the school board is still school-boarding. It was announced that the district would no longer use the word *chief* in any job titles, out of respect for Native Americans (despite the fact that the word actually comes from the French *chef*).

The other day I walked by Millennium Tower. Once a symbol of the push to transform our funky town into a big city, it's a gleaming fifty-eight-story skyscraper in the heart of San Francisco, and it's been sinking into the ground—more than a foot since it was finished in 2009. A group of men in hard hats were just standing there, staring up at it. The metaphor is obvious, but San Francisco has never been a subtle city. I'd like to believe those guys finally had a plan to fix the tower. At least they seemed to accept that it needed fixing.

For so long, San Francisco has been too self-satisfied to address the slow rot in virtually all of its institutions. But nothing's given me more hope than the rage and the recalls. "San Franciscans feel ashamed," said Michelle Tandler, a local tech worker who's documented the city's decline on social media. "I think for the first time people are like, 'Wait, what is a progressive? . . . Am I responsible? Is this my fault?'"

San Franciscans are now saying: *We can want a fairer justice system and also want to keep our car windows from getting smashed.* And: *It's not white supremacy to hope that the schools stay open, that teachers teach children, and, yes, that they test to see what those kids have learned.*

San Franciscans tricked themselves into believing that progressive politics required blocking new construction and shunning the immigrants who came to town to code. We tricked ourselves into thinking psychosis and addiction on the sidewalk were just part of the city's diversity, even as the rising

homelessness and housing prices drove out the city's actual diversity. Now residents are coming to their senses. The recalls
mean there's a limit to how far we will let the decay of this great
city go. And thank God.

Because Herb Caen was right. It's still the most beautiful city
you'll ever see.

Struggle Sessions

A struggle session is a public humiliation, and these were the years of liberals humiliating each other. They were years marked by a constant drumbeat of public defenestrations for tiny, tiny infractions. The smaller the better. It showed you were paying attention.

The modern struggle session started in the Soviet Union as the ritual of self-criticism. Vladimir Lenin in 1904 wrote about the importance of the party's "self-criticism and ruthless exposure of their own shortcomings." Under Joseph Stalin, twenty-some years later, the practice had crystallized into a set of formal rituals. "Self-criticism is a specific method, a Bolshevik method, of training the forces of the Party and of the working class generally in the spirit of revolutionary development," Stalin wrote. "Without self-criticism, our Party could not make any headway, could not disclose our ulcers, could not eliminate our shortcomings. And shortcomings we have in plenty. That must be admitted frankly and honestly."

But it was in the struggle sessions—also called denunciation rallies—in the early years of China's communist revolution when the shows really took off. "Speaking bitterness" was a way to rally support and excitement in a town, and to grow a sense of class rage. The spectacle was extraordinarily raucous. A person deemed a heretic would be denounced for reactionary thinking, sometimes by a small group, sometimes in a stadium. Groups of villagers would be gathered by party leaders, and they would be encouraged to share how they had suffered before the accused. Sessions would be emotional and chaotic, and the purpose was not just catharsis but to drum up more anger.

The photos of these sessions remain some of the most iconic images of the Cultural Revolution. Groups of young people encircle the target, who's sometimes wearing a hat or a placard. They shout out all the ways they've been hurt.

Struggle sessions had a tendency to consume everyone in their path. Even when you're in the very best standing, it's obvious that state is fragile. (As Heidi Klum said, "One day you're in. The next day you're out.") It's so hard to stay good. During the height of it, 2020 into 2021, the person performing a cancellation is often likely to be canceled. This creates a series of cancellation turduckens, a chicken in a duck in a turkey of the ousted.

As part of our cancellations, we entered an era of apologies. This may seem strange to you now, but we all got used to it. To stay in good standing required relatively frequent apologizing. It was also notable that these apologies did not help save jobs or stop criticism.

Dr. Howard Bauchner served a decade as editor in chief of the *Journal of the American Medical Association*, until JAMA posted a podcast in which two white men discussed how they believed "structural racism" was a useless term. His apology: "I once again apologize for the harms caused by this podcast and the tweet about the podcast."

People who can't apologize because they're dead are not off the hook.

"Ask if absolving Shakespeare of responsibility by mentioning that he lived at a time when hate-ridden sentiments prevailed, risks sending a subliminal message that academic excellence outweighs hateful rhetoric," wrote the author Padma Venkatraman in *School Library Journal*.

The host of the *Bachelor* franchise, Chris Harrison, had to resign after defending a contestant who'd once gone to a sorority party with an antebellum-South theme. "I am an imperfect man, I made a mistake and I own that. I believe that mistake doesn't reflect who I am or what I stand for. I am committed to progress, not just for myself, also for the franchise."

The workplace software company Slack apologized for posting about hummus while Gaza and Israel were in conflict (one that came before the recent war).

"Every year on Hummus Day, we like to share a fun little

tidbit about Slack notifications. We realize now, this year, and specifically today, was not the right time to do that. Thank you to our @SlackHQ community for holding us accountable."

A snowball of recrimination and accusation took down the most progressive candidate for the New York mayor's race in 2021, just a month before the primary. Dianne Morales, an Afro-Latina woman whose platform included "full equity for LGBTQ+/TGNCNB New Yorkers" (no idea) was canceled by her own staff. The mess included a union drive, firings of people involved in the union drive, and accusations of a toxic workplace with disappointingly "repetitive and unstructured" work. Morales staffers came to protest the office, wearing open-toed shoes and carrying tote bags as they marched. They carried signs and burned sage.

Long sessions of struggling, grieving, and apology ensued. Gina Goico, who worked on the campaign, explained: "The media and some folks are not aware of the hurt and pain these past five days the Morales Union had. Personally I feel betrayed. Gaslighted. I held Dianne in my arms while we both cried on Tuesday. I believed her."

The protestors ended the day with a group hug but also did not go to work the next day, while the candidate encouraged them to practice self-care.

Ohio State University professor Matthew J. Mayhew and student Musbah Shaheen wrote a column for *Inside Higher Ed* called "Why America Needs College Football" in September 2020. Their point: we should consider, even in a pandemic, "the essential role that college football may play toward healing a democracy made more fragile by disease, racial unrest and a contested presidential election cycle." Matthew immediately had to apologize.

Under the headline "Why America Needs College Football—Part 2," he began with an about-face: "It doesn't." His apology was lengthy and abject. "I learned that Black men putting their bodies on the line for my enjoyment is inspired and maintained by my uninformed and disconnected whiteness and, as written in my previous article, positions student athletes as white property."

"I hate that my students have to carry my ignorant racist energy with them at all times," he wrote.

Planned Parenthood, the longtime women's health organization, took to *The New York Times* to apologize for their founder's views. (Margaret Sanger's engagement with forced sterilization is a frequent right-wing talking point to undermine the organization, even though Sanger died in 1966.) But they also took time to apologize for their history of focusing on women's health. Planned Parenthood had been selfish. They had focused too much on planned parenthood.

"When we focus too narrowly on 'women's health,' we have excluded trans and nonbinary people," the organization's president wrote. "We've claimed the mantle of women's rights, to the exclusion of other causes that women of color and trans people cannot afford to ignore. And when we are rightfully called out by other leaders in the movement for reproductive justice who have pushed us for years to do better, we cry."

Her conclusion: "We must take up less space, and lend more

support. And we must put our time, energy, and resources into fights that advance an agenda other than our own."

These apologies are bold and dramatic. But an apology isn't a moment or an action, because no one is forgiven. The apology is made to everyone or no one, so it can never be accepted. So the apology now is the first step of a process that can never end—at least until everyone forgets about why they were upset. This does happen, though it's not easy for people in the midst of the struggle-session spiral to remember that the moment will pass.

Spaces needed to apologize too. Buildings needed to apologize. Land had to be acknowledged. America was taken. This land had residents before us, and we fought for it and claimed it as our own. And that also needed to be apologized for. Not that anything would be given back or changed financially. It just needed to be *acknowledged*. Like, let's remember that people were slaughtered here on the soil under this beautiful Craftsman house, and then let's continue on and have dessert.

And so we began an era of land acknowledgments. It didn't quite matter if the land had passed between different warring tribes. The idea was just to pick a tribe at random that at some point lived on this land to remind yourself that you *should apologize*. If there were multiple warring tribes, maybe pick the weaker one that was killed off by the earlier tribe. And it can be done in a playful way, as if to say, yes, these people were slaughtered and we live of their fertile earth, but they'd appreciate us.

Vancouver Island University acknowledges that we are located on the traditional and unceded territory of the Snuneymuxw People, and we thank them for allowing us to live, laugh, love, and learn here. (They later changed it.)

Harvard University is located on the traditional and ancestral land of the Massachusett.

The form usually goes like this: "Today I am speaking to you from [name of city], which is part of the unceded land of the [name of Indigenous people]. I would like to acknowledge the [name of Indigenous people] community and pay my respects to their past, present, and future elders." On Zoom meetings, it can take a while because everyone is on someone's land.

When protestors took over Seattle, they explained: "Although we have liberated Free Capitol Hill in the name of the people of Seattle, we must not forget that we stand on land already once stolen from the Duwamish People."

You're not giving the land back. You're not giving *money*. You're just saying, *Hey, I'm sorry.* And then the meeting can start.

One day, in an interview in a small-business newsletter, an up-and-coming food writer named Alison Roman saltily said that the model-turned-lifestyle influencer Chrissy Teigen and minimalism advocate Marie Kondo had gone too corporate, cranking out stuff for people to buy at Target. People were exercised and thought it suspect that Roman was after two Asian women. It didn't help that Roman did an impression, adding: "For the low, low price of $19.99, please to. . . ." Teigen tweeted a lot about it, and how she was disappointed.

Roman apologized. It wasn't deep enough. She apologized again, more fully.

"I'm a white woman who has and will continue to benefit from white privilege and I recognize that makes what I said even more inexcusable and hurtful," she wrote. As the session raged on, Roman was suspended from her column at *The New York Times*.

And then something strange happened. Pretty soon after, Chrissy Teigen got canceled.

She had apparently bullied a sixteen-year-old model named Courtney Stodden. Teigen had tweeted things at her like, "my Friday fantasy: you. dirt nap. mmm baby." Stodden, who goes by they/them pronouns, said they had gotten private messages from Teigen encouraging the teenager to kill herself. Suddenly, Teigen was toast too.

Bloomingdale's, Target, and Macy's dropped her cookware line almost instantaneously.

That's a good one. But the modern classic of the cancellation turducken, one that can be read as a parable, started in Manhattan at a magazine called *Bon Appétit* and traveled all the way to Brooklyn, to a podcast network called Gimlet Media.

Bon Appétit had been modernizing from a staid old magazine to something younger, hipper, and more diverse. But the new talent said the older, largely white staff took credit for their work and didn't promote or pay them in fair ways.

Staff wanted to oust their leader—*Bon Appétit*'s Adam Rapoport. A whistleblower found the perfect image: Rapoport had dressed for a Halloween party as a Puerto Rican in 2004. (The photograph was actually in a frame in his office.)

He and his wife both were dressed up, in fact: She had gelled her hair back and wore a pink tank top. He had on a close-fitting piece of cloth over his hair, and he had shaved his facial hair into a thin goatee. He wore a Yankees shirt, unbuttoned to reveal a heavy silver necklace that the real-life Adam Rapoport would absolutely never wear. His wife had written under the photo, damningly, "my papi."

Rapoport stepped down immediately.

He would not be returning to his nice office in One World Trade Center. His Instagram is gone and he hasn't and probably won't ever work in media again. He'll be able to find quiet, more private work, though a few years later now it's hard to tell if anyone's hired him at all. Who hires someone who resigned in a racism scandal?

That's the chicken.

The duck and turkey:

A short trip away on the 5 train is a much-loved progressive podcast company called Gimlet Media. Producers there had an idea. They would try to capture the convulsions of the culture war. They would make a podcast about the revolution at *Bon Appétit*. They would document the generational shift.

And they would do it well. Gimlet makes big productions with big teams of ambitious young podcast makers, and in these days it was the hottest podcast company around. The jewel of Gimlet is the podcast *Reply All*, which featured stories of the way the internet shapes people and vice versa. They were the perfect team to tell the story.

The host was Sruthi Pinnamaneni, a senior reporter at the company. The miniseries was called "The Test Kitchen." Pinnamaneni spent eight months reporting the story. She explained in the first episode that she would only play interviews from people of color to respect that this is not a white man's story—not Rapoport's. "The story begins with a man I have spoken to but you are not actually going to hear from him, because the story is not about him," she tells the listener. This is how they would complete the cancellation of Rapoport.

A veteran podcaster, Pinnamaneni had gone back into *Bon Appétit* history, interviewing people across ten years, and the series, she said, would show the growing pains of an organization.

After almost a year of work, two episodes aired. Before it could go further, Sruthi Pinnamaneni was herself canceled.

Her crime: She had not been properly enthusiastic about the union efforts in her own organization. And being against the union meant being against non-white Gimlet employees, according to her critics. And now she was doing a podcast about cancellations. Shouldn't someone more ethically pure do that? people were asking.

The cocreator of *Reply All*, PJ Vogt, tried to defend her. But he had also been against the union, and colleagues had started turning against him. They both were shareholders and had helped build the company, which was soon to be sold to Spotify, in a deal that would make many senior people there very wealthy. The staff revolted.

"The amount of trauma I witnessed and experienced at Gimlet as a result of those relationships of power and race is frankly incalculable," wrote Gabe, a then executive assistant at Gimlet.

"It's impossible to explain just how dark that time was," Brittany, a Gimlet host, wrote.

Within days, Pinnamaneni and Vogt had both stepped down.

The podcasters made two episodes. Then just apologies. First: "An update on the future of 'The Test Kitchen' and PJ Vogt and Sruthi Pinnamaneni's departure." Then a lot of self-criticism. In the episode called "The Test Kitchen Revisited," "the *Reply All* team takes a look at 'The Test Kitchen,' and what those mistakes mean for the future of the show." The host of the reckoning episode is the journalist Emmanuel Dzotsi. He brings on Alex Goldman, who is still on the team at that point. Goldman is there to say sorry.

"What we want to do is apologize. We really hurt a lot of people. We hurt people from *Bon Appétit*, we hurt our colleagues, and we hurt our listeners. We are very, very sorry."

Dzotsi then reads the apology statement from Sruthi, who will never be heard from again on Gimlet.

"Quote: My reporting on *Bon Appétit* helped me recognize my own mistakes in the workplace, but not clearly enough and not soon enough to fully reckon with them."

Alex then read the apology statement from PJ.

"Quote: I didn't support the Gimlet Union. At the time, I

didn't believe it was the best choice for me personally. That was the wrong call, and I'm sorry for it. What I didn't consider then, and I wish I had, was what the union represented to people of color at the company. Seeing how much hurt and disappointment people felt about my choice, I decided the best way to hold myself accountable was to step down."

Dzotsi wraps it up.

"So that's what PJ and Sruthi had to say about the mistakes that they've made. After looking through a lot of these mistakes we made the decision not to air the last two episodes of 'The Test Kitchen' series. . . . I'm thinking about who remains and what remains. What is left of this show? What is *Reply All* now?"

That fateful photo of Rapoport in Puerto Rican garb had originally been resurfaced on social media by Tammie Teclemariam, a food writer. When all the dominos had fallen and the editor was out and the podcast hosts were out, Tammie talked to *The New York Times* to mull her handiwork. "Being 'cancel-adjacent' is exhausting," she said. "If we cancel everyone, who will be left?"

PJ Vogt disappeared for a while. His digital footprint was frozen in permanent apology. He started an infrequent blog, meekly called *Proof of Life*. "I am not, at present, writing a classic American novel," he wrote. "I am not writing a megahit bestseller about how I found myself. At this point, I'm not even making a podcast. If I'm honest with you, right now just writing this tiny newsletter is not particularly easy for me. Writing feels uncomfortable."

Then, not so much later, he came back with a self-produced podcast about the crypto bubble. It was well received. He slowly began posting again, though mostly in private, like someone with PTSD. He launched another podcast.

Sruthi Pinnamaneni disappeared a little. She deleted her Twitter; online, there's an old bare-bones personal website but no Sruthi Pinnamaneni LinkedIn profile. Just a few news stories about how she was canceled. But she didn't die. She quietly took on other work.

Chrissy Teigen's cookware was never picked up again by Bloomingdale's and Macy's after they dropped her—not that she's in any tough financial straits.

The real lesson, though, is the chef. Alison Roman actually powered through her long snowstorm of cancellation and eventually came out the other side. Her newsletter and videos grew more and more popular. She owns her own recipes now, even had a nice gig at the big-ticket misfire that was CNN+. But the place that helped make her name and then promptly kicked her to the curb at the first sign of trouble, *The New York Times*, hasn't had a Roman byline since and likely never will, not least because she doesn't need them now.

Well. She actually reengaged with the *Times* in 2023. There was a public letter going around calling out by name several reporters who were "following the lead of far-right hate groups" for the way they covered trans issues. It was basically an effort to cancel these reporters. The workplace was "hostile by bias." It was funny to see Roman signed on.

The Joy of Canceling

The first time I was consciously part of canceling someone, it felt incredible. I do remember the pleasure.

The situation was pretty clear-cut: A close friend was canceling someone. And I could help.

My friend was a prominent black writer and hilarious person, and she was quoted in a book. I knew the author too, who was a white woman, also well known, less hilarious but equally lovely. I'd met her at a couple parties and liked her. She had asked me to do an onstage interview with her as part of her book tour, which I'd been thrilled to do. It would be at a tech campus, and I'd be doing a fun casual interview onstage. The event was announced and posted online.

Then came the fight.

My friend didn't like the quote when it came out in the book. She posted to her sizable Twitter followers about it. She said the author hadn't told her she was on the record (the author disagreed). She said she was misquoted and also had no idea she was being interviewed (the author disagreed). It was a shit show. And in the court of public opinion: my friend was winning.

Good.

It was playing out on Twitter, which sounds silly and light. *It's Twitter, not real life,* is the phrase people say. But for the media class—the people who decide what books go on tour and what books get reviewed, what books you hear about, what books show up at the tech campus circuit—it's the artery system. And the author was getting dragged. Then of course the articles come out about it. Twitter is where stories get ginned up.

A drumbeat of rage was growing against the author. I felt the rage too. Like seeing someone flagrantly litter or snatch a purse, she'd violated the contract we all made. And her apology had been defensive. If we'd learned anything from anti-racist school, it's that apologies had to be abject and endless. She was pushing back still, a little. My disgust grew.

The author was an obnoxious white woman taking what wasn't hers, words she didn't get consent to write down, or maybe even words that were never said in the first place. The people I loved were disgusted by her, and so was I. We were circling the wagons. We were saying *enough is enough*. White women can't just take words from a black woman to sell shitty books! The premise of her book was vile anyway. The author was vile. Black lives very much matter and a random white liberal needs to know that.

I joined in hard. My friend never asked me to do anything, but I wanted to do something to defend her. A good ally is assertive and doesn't need to be asked. A good ally seeks out opportunities like this. Platforming, sitting on stage with her, was endorsing her. I wanted to embarrass the author, and I could.

I wrote the author and said I was sorry but I could no longer participate in her book tour. I couldn't help her promote this book. I wouldn't be able to sit onstage with her for any reason. She'd need to find someone else. She asked me to reconsider. I wouldn't.

I told a lot of friends about that. I wanted people to know about it. I was proud. People said I'd done the right thing, but I didn't need to hear it from them.

The author existed in our community. She went to the parties I went to and showed up at the same events as me. The goal was to slice her carefully out, and I was thrilled to do my part. To let someone stay like that is to allow rot. By showing where I stood, I felt closer to my friends. But also, in some ways, doing what I did is the price of admission. To ignore the drumbeat was to suggest that I didn't care. I definitely did care.

I saw later that the event was canceled altogether after I withdrew. Her book tour didn't work so well. The book didn't sell so well. I never saw her at another party, and I never heard from her again, and I was fine with that.

To do a cancellation is a very warm, social thing. It has the energy of a potluck. Everyone brings what they can, and everyone is impressed by the creativity of their friends. It's a positive thing, what you're doing, and it doesn't feel like battle so much as nurturing the love for one's friends, tending the warm fire of a cause. You have real power when you're doing it. And with enough people, you can oust someone very powerful.

The easy criticism of a cancellation is: You went after someone who agrees with you on almost everything but some minor tiny differences? Some small infraction? It seems bizarre. But that's the point. The bad among us are more dangerous to the group. Mormons don't excommunicate a random drag performer. They excommunicate a bad Mormon. I'd watched all the presidential debates in 2016 with some family members, who are conservatives. After Hillary lost, I couldn't stomach going over there for a few months. I was too upset, and I couldn't handle seeing them happy. But that's not a cancellation. I had no power over these family members or sway in their community. I couldn't make them apologize for being happy that Trump won.

A cancellation isn't about finding a conservative and yelling at them. It's about finding the betrayer in your midst. It's about sniffing them out at your coffee shop or your office. They look and talk like you. They blend in perfectly. But they're not like you.

One day, there was a woman I tried to cancel but failed at spectacularly. She was hired as a colleague at the *Times* and was already a known *heterodox*. She came along with an older conservative guy, both from *The Wall Street Journal*, both then to our Opinion pages. I wrote to their boss to complain about the hires. When the editor in chief was in town, I made sure to ask him in front of our team why these two had been hired. This was before 2020 and the riots and before I realized that my movement would try to eat its own. This was when I was one of the people helming things.

Then I happened to be in New York one day. The young heterodox writer sent me an idea for a story, and I said since I'm in town maybe we should get coffee. I told my editor I was going to set her politics straight.

I don't know what to say other than that when we met, I fell in love immediately. I knew immediately. Our early dates were fights about politics, and I couldn't get enough. But this wasn't allowed within the movement. The personal is political. I pretended like that wasn't true and that I could ignore it and remain in good standing. Being with her didn't change my beliefs. I still wanted universal health care, I would say, a sort of incantation. But the movement was a social one. It's not a checklist of policies and whether you believe yay or nay. Falling in love with someone outside the community made me suspect. And most damningly it made me soft.

Because around my thirtieth birthday, there came a day when I didn't cancel someone, and it was the true end of my time in the movement. Reporting on the wrong topics had gotten me close. But it was resisting a cancellation that did me in.

I knew the thing I was meant to yell about that day. I knew the tweet I was meant to send, but I liked the target too much. He was sweet and younger than me. I was agonized over it, sweating in my apartment. I sometimes get this bizarre psychosomatic stress response where my arms go limp in a panic, and all that day my arms were going limp. I got a few notes pushing me to join in. It was important. We had to draw a line that day. We had to speak in unison. My voice needed to bolster the other voices.

I just couldn't bring myself to do it. I didn't think the violation was so bad. I'd gotten old or soft or something, and there I was, too pathetic and limp-armed to even send a nasty tweet.

Eventually that close friend of mine from the book circled back to me. The one I had canceled in honor of. We'd lived together at one point when we were both coming up in the world, cooked together, talked about our families, plotted our careers together. Both our lives came to fruition as we'd planned them, and there was a thrill in that with each other. I loved this friend and still do. But I knew what was coming when I saw her name on my phone.

She said very nicely that it was suspicious how quiet I was that day. She said, *Nellie, you say a lot of things, yet you haven't said anything about this one, today.* She very politely told me that I was a racist.

Then she said goodbye.

We could trace this moment of scolding and overcorrections, of panics and irrationality, and pretend to come up with some

235

clean, distinct intellectual history for how it came about. We could say, oh yes, it all started in the 1960s with Michel Foucault and the French critical theorists who argued (convincingly) that there were no absolutes, that everything was constructed and could be deconstructed, that Marxism was a social program as much as an economic one—an argument that was very successful in American universities.

We could say it's just that our society got decadent. With plenty of food and shelter and no real threats of violence day-to-day, we became obsessed with minutiae and linguistic games. That's the one I think of as the allergy hypothesis. Our minds need battle. Evolution's prepared us for survival. And so when large threats disappear, the mind goes hunting for smaller ones. (She likes *that* tweet?)

But what I think now is this is just the human condition. We were always like this. We're monkeys. We get overexcited and irrational and tribal. Satanic panics come and go. That's our nature. Everything else is the challenge. Liberalism, tolerance, living among and working with people we disagree with? That is what is completely unnatural.

The years I spent reporting this book—the early 2020s—happened to be the start of the revolution. The first phase was ending as I wrapped this. The movement leaders were sneaking off with funds gathered in the height of rage, settling into pretty canyons. The rallying cries were being deleted from websites and memories. (No one ever said *abolish the police*, I've been told recently.) The word *woke* had gotten exhausting. It sounded dated.

Black Lives Matter was in disgrace. All the autonomous zones had shuttered. The police were re-funded. The Tavistock pediatric gender clinic in England where children would be assessed and begin their transitions? That's shutting down. And then came the lawsuits. Many young adults started suing the doctors who'd treated them as adolescents. Businesses were suing the cities.

But did the quieter streets mean it was done? Hardly. The ideas became the operating principle of big business, the tech company handbook, the head of HR, the statement you have to write to get a job in a university. The movement fell apart because of how fully it succeeded. It didn't need to announce itself so loudly anymore. We didn't need to notice it anymore.

Schools in Evanston, Illinois, outside Chicago, were offering racially segregated high school math and writing classes, and it was no longer a big or shocking story. It's voluntary, they say, so it's legal. There are a thousand tiny changes we've just grown accustomed to.

I think about the parts I loved at the start of the fragile, hopeful movement that really did bring new ideas into the world. Ideas around fairness, around language, around our bodies. The revolution believed in profound, almost violent empathy, and it believed that life could be gentle and easy if we spoke just a little differently and walked just a little softer. The revolution said your DNA could be rewired in your mind. It said we could all live in peace if the authorities just left us alone for a while. I don't think I'll be around a group so optimistic again in my life.

By the time I was finishing these chapters, new forces were coming up, rattling around. A youthful post-woke community promising to bring back shock and fun. A resurgent New Right was announcing a return to something, to sun and muscles and tradwives, to that imagined Bronze Age traditionalism, to Catholicism. It's tapping into old ideas and old rages, lit anew by the revolution. And a hemming-and-hawing moderate like myself is its enemy, just as much as we are the enemy of the progressive. The New Right says, "Look, your movement, all your rights, that's where this started." The movement says moderate liberals will always descend into chaotic extremes. Some of them say that gay marriage is when the slide began. Some say it started with women getting the right to vote.

Rising also was the new focus on Israel and Jews. Hamas soldiers became heroes of the Left. Dozens of early leaders within the Democratic Socialists of America disavowed the organization as it spun deeper into obsession with eliminating the Jewish state. At the University of Wisconsin–Madison, after a terrorist attack against Israel, students gathered for a call-and-response that went like this:

Glory to the martyrs!

Response: *Glory to the resistance!*

We will liberate the land!

Response: *By any means necessary!*

My own cancellation was never formalized. But I heard

enough of the drumbeat—*Why do you think it's OK to murder black people, Nellie?* is a text I have gotten—to know what was coming. And I kept thinking about my conservative family members and how I couldn't cancel them because they didn't operate by those rules—and also because, truth be told, I loved them. To be canceled and to participate in the cancellation, someone has to care very deeply and need the love of that group or need the jobs that group provides. And my family members didn't. I didn't either. I fell in love with that heterodox writer. I couldn't help myself. I couldn't prioritize the political over the personal. I couldn't be a good soldier. I couldn't unsee the complexity and absurdity.

I slowly started easing out. Socially, tentatively. Financially, tentatively.

I never heard from my friend again after she said goodbye. I get it. She's drawing the line. Part of me admires her for it.

THE END

Acknowledgments

First, I'd like to thank the people in this book. Those named and those anonymized. I'm glad to be born in such interesting times with all of you.

Many, many people helped me become a writer. My teachers at Hamlin and Cate School, my editors and mentors at the *San Francisco Chronicle*. But for this book in particular: I'd like to thank my former boss at *The New York Times*, Pui-Wing Tam. She took a chance on a local San Francisco reporter and brought me to the big league, knowing there was a nonzero chance I would then send up the big league. She is calm yet fierce, and I'm so grateful for her. Thanks to Choire Sicha, whose humor and story sense are unmatched. He might deny that he helped edit this book, but he did. Thank you also to Ellen Pollock and Nick Summers.

Thank you to Jeffrey Goldberg and Honor Jones at *The Atlantic* for making the San Francisco story shine.

Thank you to my agents, Keith Urbahn and Matt Latimer, who were so refreshing to discover. Thank you to my book editor, Bria Sandford, who reached out to me when I was feeling crazy and said maybe that crazy could be a book. Her patience is unmatched.

Thank you to Caitlin Flanagan for her friendship, wisdom, and onion dip. Thank you to Suzy Weiss for her early reads and punch-ups. And thank you to Sue Carswell for the eagle-eyed read and taking such good care of these pages.

Thank you to our nanny, Maria, whose time caring for our daughter allowed me the time to write this. And thank you to that sweet child. I can't wait to watch you grow up and decide whether you'll cancel us from the right or from the left. The world is your oyster, my love.

Thank you to my friends who've given my life so much joy. I'm lucky in life because I've been able to walk it with all of you. I won't list everyone. But you know who you are.

Thank you to my parents—all four, Demi and Tom, Henry and Jennifer—and Uncle Bill (so, I'll say five altogether) for raising me to be free and independent. Dad, you taught me that if things seem irrational, then they probably are, and it's okay to laugh about it. Mom, I could not and would not have finished this if it weren't for you. Thank you to my Uncle Ted and Mary for being the best home for debates and cozy nights. To the late uncle Richard for opening my mind, and to Tanta Bea for showing me how to make a little magic in life. Thank you to my uncle Philip, who is the funniest writer in the family. I'm grateful for all my cousins, Georgis and Bowles, who bring fun to every holiday and make me so proud to be part of these families. And thank you to my brothers and sisters: Henry, George, Charlotte, James, Chris, and Diana.

And thank you most of all to my wife, Bari. You've given me a life and a love I couldn't have imagined.